Ginn Mathematics

TEXTBOOK 1

C000161789

GINN

Which operations?

Addition, subtraction, multiplication and division are called **operations** on numbers.

The numbers have been blotted out in the following problems. You don't need them. What you have to do is to write down the operations that are needed to find the answers.

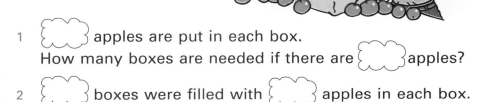

1   {   } apples are put in each box.
    How many boxes are needed if there are {   } apples?

2   {   } boxes were filled with {   } apples in each box.
    How many many apples have been packed?

Two operations are needed in the following questions. Give them in their correct order.

3   The price of a TV set was {50} pounds.
    It was reduced by {4} pounds, but no-one bought it.
    The shopkeeper then halved this price and sold the set.
    How much was it sold for?

4   Dave's grandfather is {10} times as old as Dave.
    Dave's age is {5}.
    How old was the grandfather {3} years ago?

5

    {40} chairs were being placed in a hall for a concert.
    {4} were found to be broken.

    The other chairs were put in {6} rows with the same numbers in each row.

    How many chairs were there in each row?

Finding a fraction of a number.

To find $\frac{1}{2}$ of a number, divide by 2.

$\frac{1}{2}$ of 8 = 4

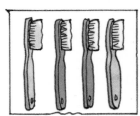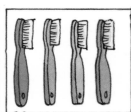

Here's how to find $\frac{2}{3}$ of a number.

Step 1. Divide by 3 to find $\frac{1}{3}$.
$12 \div 3 = 4$

Step 2. Multiply the result from **Step 1** by 2 to find $\frac{2}{3}$.
$4 \times 2 = 8$
$\frac{2}{3}$ of 12 = 8

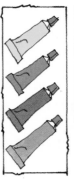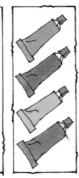

1   Copy and complete the equations:

(a) $\frac{1}{2}$ of 12 = ___

(b) $\frac{1}{3}$ of 9 = ___

(c) $\frac{3}{4}$ of 12 = ___

(d) $\frac{3}{4}$ of 20 = ___

2   (a) $\frac{1}{4}$ of 8 = ___   (b) $\frac{1}{5}$ of 25 = ___   (c) $\frac{1}{5}$ of 35 = ___   (d) $\frac{1}{3}$ of 21 = ___

(e) $\frac{1}{4}$ of 28 = ___   (f) $\frac{1}{2}$ of 6 = ___   (g) $\frac{1}{8}$ of 24 = ___   (h) $\frac{1}{5}$ of 40 = ___

3   (a) $\frac{2}{3}$ of 9 = ___   (b) $\frac{2}{3}$ of 48 = ___   (c) $\frac{5}{8}$ of 48 = ___   (d) $\frac{3}{4}$ of 16 = ___

(e) $\frac{3}{5}$ of 40 = ___   (f) $\frac{2}{3}$ of 15 = ___   (g) $\frac{3}{4}$ of 8 = ___   (h) $\frac{2}{3}$ of 24 = ___

4 (a) $\frac{1}{3}$ of 18 = ___   (b) $\frac{2}{3}$ of 18 = ___   (c) $\frac{3}{3}$ of 18 = ___

5 (a) $\frac{1}{4}$ of 20 = ___   (b) $\frac{2}{4}$ of 20 = ___   (c) $\frac{3}{4}$ of 20 = ___

6 (a) $\frac{1}{5}$ of 30 = ___   (b) $\frac{2}{5}$ of 30 = ___   (c) $\frac{3}{5}$ of 30 = ___

7 (a) $\frac{1}{6}$ of 42 = ___   (b) $\frac{1}{8}$ of 40 = ___   (c) $\frac{3}{8}$ of 24 = ___

(d) $\frac{3}{8}$ of 8 = ___   (e) $\frac{5}{6}$ of 36 = ___   (f) $\frac{5}{8}$ of 32 = ___

(g) $\frac{5}{6}$ of 30 = ___   (h) $\frac{7}{8}$ of 16 = ___   (i) $\frac{5}{9}$ of 18 = ___

You pay only $\frac{2}{3}$ of the marked price.

£24.00

$\frac{1}{3}$ of £24.00 = £8.00

so $\frac{2}{3}$ of £24.00 = £16.00

8 Find the sale price.

(a) You pay only $\frac{3}{4}$ of the marked price.

(b) You pay only $\frac{3}{4}$ of the marked price.

(c) You pay only $\frac{2}{3}$ of the marked price.

£36.00

£32.00

£27.00

9 Sally went on a 15 kilometre hike. At the end of 3 hours she had hiked $\frac{2}{3}$ of the way. How many kilometres had she hiked?

10 Jack had £12.00. He spent $\frac{2}{3}$ of it on a camping knife. Later, he bought a kettle for £3.99. How much money did he have left

Equivalent fractions.

$\frac{3}{8}$ ← The number at the top is the **numerator**.
← The number at the bottom is the **denominator**.

These pictures show that $\frac{3}{8}$ is the same fraction as $\frac{6}{16}$.

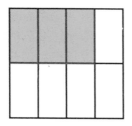
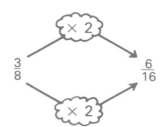
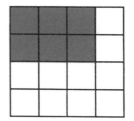

1   Copy and complete the equations. You don't have to draw the pictures.

(a) 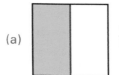 $\frac{1}{2} =$ ——

(b) $\frac{1}{3} =$ ——

(c) 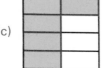 $\frac{5}{8} =$ ——

(d) $\frac{5}{6} =$ ——

(e) 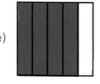 $\frac{4}{5} =$ ——

(f) $\frac{2}{3} =$ ——

(g) $\frac{3}{4} =$ ——

(h) $\frac{4}{4} =$ ——

If you multiply or divide the numerator and denominator of a fraction by the same number (not 0), you get an **equivalent** fraction.

Examples $\frac{4}{5} = \frac{4 \times 2}{5 \times 2} = \frac{8}{10}$ $\frac{4}{5} = \frac{4 \times 3}{5 \times 3} = \frac{12}{15}$ $\frac{4}{5} = \frac{4 \times 4}{5 \times 4} = \frac{16}{20}$

2 Copy and complete these to give equivalent fractions.

(a) $\dfrac{7}{8} = \dfrac{}{}$ (×10)

(b) $\dfrac{3}{10} = \dfrac{}{}$ (×9)

(c) $\dfrac{4}{6} = \dfrac{}{}$ (×8)

(d) $\dfrac{7}{7} = \dfrac{}{}$ (×6)

(e) $\dfrac{7}{10} = \dfrac{}{}$ (×2)

(f) $\dfrac{1}{20} = \dfrac{}{}$ (×7)

(g) $\dfrac{2}{9} = \dfrac{}{}$ (×10)

(h) $\dfrac{4}{8} = \dfrac{}{}$ (×9)

3 Copy and complete:

(a) $\dfrac{3}{5} = \dfrac{}{15}$

(b) $\dfrac{2}{3} = \dfrac{}{9}$

(c) $\dfrac{5}{8} = \dfrac{}{24}$

(d) $\dfrac{1}{9} = \dfrac{}{36}$

(e) $\dfrac{3}{5} = \dfrac{12}{}$

(f) $\dfrac{2}{3} = \dfrac{14}{}$

(g) $\dfrac{5}{8} = \dfrac{20}{}$

(h) $\dfrac{1}{9} = \dfrac{5}{}$

4 (a) Find a fraction equivalent to $\frac{4}{5}$ that has a numerator of 20.

(b) Find a fraction equivalent to $\frac{4}{9}$ that has a denominator of 27.

5 Copy and complete this sequence to find eight fractions that are equivalent to $\frac{2}{5}$.

$\dfrac{2 \times 2}{5 \times 2} = \dfrac{4}{10}$ $\dfrac{2 \times 3}{5 \times 3} = \dfrac{6}{15}$ $\dfrac{2 \times 4}{5 \times 4} = \dfrac{}{}$ $\dfrac{2 \times 5}{5 \times 5} = \dfrac{}{}$

$\dfrac{2 \times 6}{5 \times 6} = \dfrac{}{}$ $\dfrac{2 \times 7}{5 \times 7} = \dfrac{}{}$ $\dfrac{2 \times }{5 \times } = \dfrac{}{}$ $\dfrac{2 \times }{5 \times } = \dfrac{}{}$

6 Use the method of question 5 to find nine fractions that are equivalent to $\frac{3}{4}$.

7 Start with any three simple fractions, and see how many equivalents you can find.
Work with a friend, and give yourselves a time limit (say, five minutes).
Use your calculator if you like.

Reducing fractions.

If you divide the numerator and denominator of a fraction by
the same number, you get an equivalent fraction.

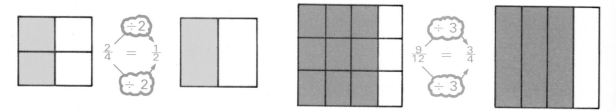

Notice that the answer is a fraction with a smaller numerator and denominator.
This is called **reducing a fraction to lower terms.**
A fraction that cannot be reduced to lower terms is in **lowest terms.**

1   Copy and complete the equations.

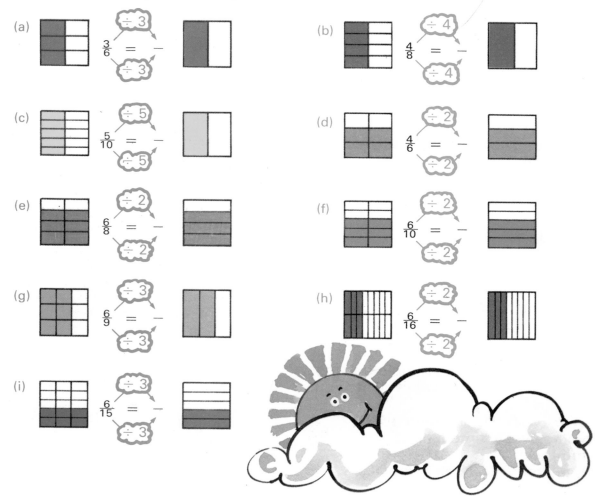

2 Copy and complete:

(a) $\frac{3}{9} = $ —

(b) $\frac{6}{12} = $ —

(c) $\overset{\div 3}{\frown}$ $\frac{3}{12} = $ —

(d) $\overset{\div 5}{\frown}$ $\frac{10}{15} = $ —

(e) $\overset{\div 3}{\frown}$ $\frac{4}{12} = $ — $\overset{\div 4}{\frown}$

(f) $\overset{\div 6}{\frown}$ $\frac{10}{16} = $ — $\overset{\div 2}{\frown}$ think!

(g) $\overset{\div 3}{\frown}$ think! $\frac{12}{16} = $ — $\overset{\div 4}{\frown}$

(h) $\overset{\div 5}{\frown}$ think! $\frac{8}{8} = $ — $\overset{\div 8}{\frown}$

Reduce these to lowest terms.

3 (a) $\frac{4}{16}$ (b) $\frac{10}{12}$ (c) $\frac{15}{20}$ (d) $\frac{24}{36}$ (e) $\frac{15}{25}$ (f) $\frac{15}{30}$

   (g) $\frac{16}{24}$ (h) $\frac{16}{18}$ (i) $\frac{12}{18}$ (j) $\frac{8}{16}$ (k) $\frac{9}{24}$ (l) $\frac{6}{24}$

4 (a) $\frac{9}{36}$ (b) $\frac{8}{24}$ (c) $\frac{18}{27}$ (d) $\frac{18}{24}$ (e) $\frac{42}{56}$ (f) $\frac{35}{40}$

   (g) $\frac{27}{36}$ (h) $\frac{24}{48}$ (i) $\frac{72}{81}$ (j) $\frac{56}{72}$ (k) $\frac{48}{56}$ (l) $\frac{40}{56}$

5 (a) $\frac{80}{100}$ (b) $\frac{76}{100}$ (c) $\frac{21}{98}$ (d) $\frac{28}{56}$ (e) $\frac{77}{110}$ (f) $\frac{48}{120}$

What is my number?

6 (a)

My number is equivalent to $\frac{2}{3}$. The denominator is 6.

(b)

My number is equivalent to $\frac{3}{4}$. The numerator is 12.

(c)

My number is equivalent to $\frac{12}{18}$. The denominator is 6.

(d)

My number is equivalent to $\frac{16}{24}$. It is in lowest terms.

Multiplying a three-digit number.

Multiply 369 by 2.

```
  369
×   2
   18      (9 × 2 =   18)
  120      (60 × 2 = 120)
  600      (300 × 2 = 600)
  738
```

Here is a shorter way. First multiply units and regroup.

```
  369
×   2
    8
```

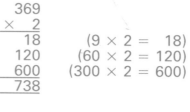

Multiply tens, add and regroup.

```
  369
×   2
   38
```

Finally multiply hundreds and add.

```
  369
×   2
  738
```

Copy and complete.

1 (a)
```
  214
×   2
```
(b)
```
  303
×   3
```
(c)
```
  323
×   2
```
(d)
```
  121
×   4
```
(e)
```
  102
×   4
```

2 (a)
```
  324
×   3
```
(b)
```
  216
×   4
```
(c)
```
  103
×   5
```
(d)
```
  222
×   4
```
(e)
```
  111
×   6
```

3 (a)
```
  152
×   4
```
(b)
```
  261
×   3
```
(c)
```
  150
×   4
```
(d)
```
  141
×   5
```
(e)
```
  231
×   4
```

4 (a) 126 (b) 196 (c) 178 (d) 159 (e) 138
      × 4   × 5   × 6   × 8   × 4

5 (a) 168 (b) 167 (c) 126 (d) 284 (e) 296
      × 5   × 5   × 3   × 3   × 3

6 (a) 157 (b) 287 (c) 175 (d) 359 (e) 248
      × 5   × 3   × 4   × 2   × 3

7 (a) 375 (b) 146 (c) 129 (d) 137 (e) 159
      × 2   × 6   × 3   × 8   × 7

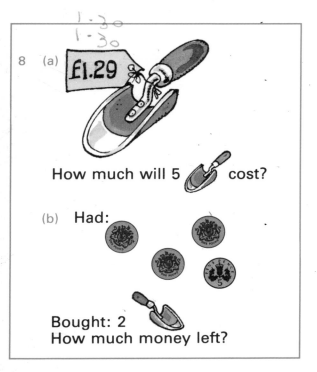

8 (a) £1.29
How much will 5 cost?

(b) Had:

Bought: 2
How much money left?

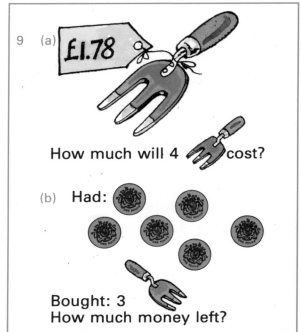

9 (a) £1.78
How much will 4 cost?

(b) Had:

Bought: 3
How much money left?

10 A gardener bought
4 plants costing £1.63 each.

(a) What is the total cost?

(b) How much change would
he have from £10.00?

11 What is the total cost of
5 shrubs costing £1.36 each
and 3 trees costing £2.87 each?

More about multiplying a three-digit number.

Multiply 538 by 6.

```
  538
×   6
   48      (8 × 6 = 48)
  180     (30 × 6 = 180)
 3000    (500 × 6 = 3000)
 3228
```

 Multiply units and regroup.

 Multiply tens, add and regroup.

Multiply hundreds and add.

32 hundreds, or 3 thousands and 2 hundreds.

1 (a) 358   (b) 643   (c) 482   (d) 952   (e) 554
       × 5   × 4   × 6   × 3   × 2

2 (a) 683   (b) 397   (c) 749   (d) 376   (e) 874
       × 7   × 8   × 5   × 7   × 9

3 (a) 853   (b) 493   (c) 256   (d) 800   (e) 700
       × 4   × 9   × 8   × 9   × 7

4 Give each product.

   (a) 264 × 3   (b) 526 × 5   (c) 387 × 4   (d) 706 × 7

5 Multiply across. Multiply down. The first one is done for you.

   (a)

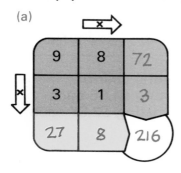

   (b)

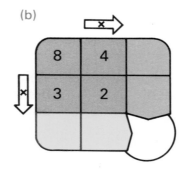

   (c)

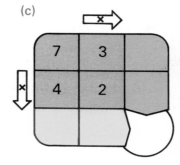

We can use rounding to estimate a product.
An estimate can tell us whether our answer makes sense.

$$\begin{array}{r} 417 \\ \times\ 7 \\ \hline \end{array}$$
Round to
$$\begin{array}{r} 400 \\ \times\ 7 \\ \hline 2800 \end{array}$$

So the product is about 2800.

$$\begin{array}{r} 417 \\ \times\ 7 \\ \hline 2919 \end{array}$$
Our answer is quite close to 2800 so it makes sense.

6   First estimate the product, then multiply.

(a) $\begin{array}{r} 78 \\ \times\ 9 \\ \hline \end{array}$ (b) $\begin{array}{r} 94 \\ \times\ 8 \\ \hline \end{array}$ (c) $\begin{array}{r} 766 \\ \times\ 5 \\ \hline \end{array}$ (d) $\begin{array}{r} 911 \\ \times\ 7 \\ \hline \end{array}$ (e) $\begin{array}{r} 835 \\ \times\ 6 \\ \hline \end{array}$

(f) 396×5 (g) 784×6 (h) 923×8

7   How much for 4 kg?

8   How much for 3 tickets?

9   A jet aeroplane, averaged 916 kilometres per hour for a 3 hour flight. How many kilometres was the flight?

10   A pair of jeans costs £12.79. How much do 3 pairs cost?

11   Find the cost of some of your clothes.
Make up multiplication problems like the one in question 10.
Give them to a friend to solve.
Your friend can make up some problems for you.

The four operations with brackets (1).

Find the value of (158 × 3) + 174.
Remember to work out the brackets first.

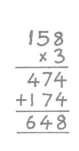

$$
\begin{array}{r}
158 \\
\times 3 \\
\hline
474 \\
+174 \\
\hline
648
\end{array}
$$

1   Work these out.

(a)   (78 × 3) + 14

(b)   70 × (3 + 14)

(c)   (167 × 5) − 2

(d)   167 × (5 − 2)

(e)   (532 − 4) × 2

(f)   532 − (4 ÷ 2)

(g)   (821 × 5) + 253

(h)   (816 × 2) + 4816

(i)   (621 − 387) × 6

(j)   (713 + 281) × 2

Hint: Each problem has two steps; use brackets.

2   Mitzi bought 2 blouses for £5.50 each and a pair of jeans for £14.99.
What was the total cost?

3   Alan bought a jumper for £8.99 and a pair of jeans for £10.99.
He gave the shop assistant £20.00.
How much change did he get back?

4   Phil could buy 3 pairs of socks for £2.40 and a jumper for £7.50.
How much would 1 pair of socks and a jumper cost?

5   Helen bought 3 shirts for £6.49 each. She gave the shop assistant £20.00.
How much change did she get back?

6   Make up some questions of your own, like questions 2 to 5.
All the questions should be designed so that you need to use brackets to work them out.
Give your questions to a friend to work out.
See if you can work out your friend's questions.

Multiplication Game.

Build the greatest product.

1.
```
  7 6 4
×     8
─────────
6 1 1 2
  5 3
```

```
  8 6 4
×     7
─────────
6 0 4 8
  4 1
```

1.
```
  5 0 3
×     8
─────────
```

```
  8 3 0
×     5
─────────
```

2.
```
  5 7 6
×     9
─────────
```

```
  9 6 7
×     5
─────────
```

3.
```
  7 3 8
×     4
─────────
```

```
  4 8 3
×     7
─────────
```

4.
```
  9 4 3
×     6
─────────
```

```
  6 3 4
×     9
─────────
```

Play the game.

A   This game is for two or more players.
    Prepare two sets of ten cards with a different digit on each
    (0, 1, 2, 3, 4, 5, 6, 7, 8, 9).
    Mix up the cards.

B   Choose a leader.

C   Each player draws a table
    like the following:

D   Without looking, the leader picks a card.
    Each player writes the digit in any box in his or her table.

E   Repeat **D** until all four boxes are filled.

F   Multiply. The player who builds the greatest answer or 'product' wins
    the game.

Investigating number patterns.

Here is an interesting number pattern.

$$(0 \times 9) + 1 = 1$$
$$(1 \times 9) + 2 = 11$$
$$(12 \times 9) + 3 = \underline{}$$
$$(123 \times 9) + 4 = \underline{}$$
$$(1234 \times 9) + 5 = \underline{}$$

1   Use a calculator to find the missing answers.

2   (a) What do you think the next three equations in the pattern would be?

     (b) What do you think the answers will be?
You should be able to say just by looking at the pattern.

     (c) Check by using a calculator.

3   Does the pattern continue further?

4   Investigate this number pattern in the same way.
Answer questions 1 to 3 for this pattern.

$$(0 \times 9) + 8 = \underline{}$$
$$(9 \times 9) + 8 = \underline{}$$
$$(98 \times 9) + 8 = \underline{}$$
$$(987 \times 9) + 8 = \underline{}$$
$$(9876 \times 9) + 8 = \underline{}$$

Dividing a three-digit number by a single-digit number.

The example shows how to divide a 3-digit number by a 1-digit number.

3)448
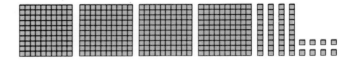

Step 1. Divide hundreds. Subtract.

```
     1
3)448
 -300
  148
```
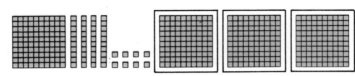

Step 2. Regroup 1 hundred for 10 tens.

```
     1
3)448
 -300
  148
```
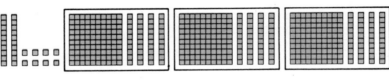

Step 3. Divide tens. Subtract.

```
    14
3)448
 -300
  148
 -120
   28
```
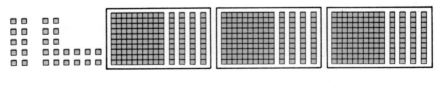

Step 4. Regroup 2 tens for 20 units.

```
    14
3)448
 -300
  148
 -120
   28
```
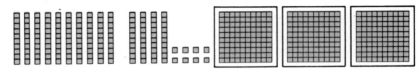

Step 5. Divide units. Subtract.

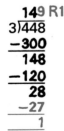

```
  149 R1
3)448
 -300
  148
 -120
   28
  -27
    1
```
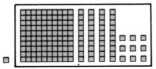 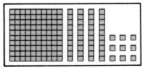 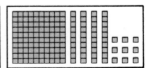

Divide.

1 (a) $3\overline{)527}$ (b) $4\overline{)952}$ (c) $2\overline{)504}$ (d) $5\overline{)745}$ (e) $2\overline{)963}$

   (f) $2\overline{)856}$ (g) $5\overline{)742}$ (h) $6\overline{)629}$ (i) $4\overline{)859}$ (j) $3\overline{)398}$

2 (a) $749 \div 7$ (b) $900 \div 8$ (c) $378 \div 2$ (d) $842 \div 6$ (e) $726 \div 4$

   (f) $953 \div 4$ (g) $974 \div 9$ (h) $627 \div 3$ (i) $700 \div 2$ (j) $958 \div 9$

3 (a) $2\overline{)£4.76}$ (b) $7\overline{)£8.96}$ (c) $8\overline{)£8.08}$ (d) $3\overline{)£5.34}$ (e) $5\overline{)£8.85}$

4 (a) The Adams family drove
       360 kilometres in 5 hours.
       How many kilometres did they
       average each hour?

   (b) The Adams' car averaged
       8 kilometres per litre of petrol.
       How many litres of petrol did
       they use on the 360-kilometre
       journey?

5 Copy and complete these division problems.

(a)
```
      _ 6 8 R1
  2)_ 3 _
   -4 0 0
    1 3 _
   -1 2 _
      1 _
    - _ _
      _
```

(b)
```
      1 _ 5 R5
  6)_ _ _
   -_ 0 0
    2 7 _
   -_ _ _
      3 _
     -3 _
      _
```

Division of a three-digit number with regrouping.

Sometimes you have to regroup before you start dividing.

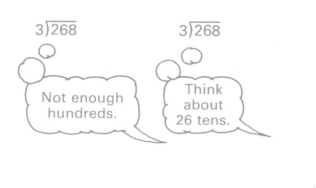

$$3\overline{)268}$$

Not enough hundreds.

$$3\overline{)268}$$

Think about 26 tens.

$$\begin{array}{r} 89\ R1 \\ 3\overline{)268} \\ -240 \\ \hline 28 \\ -27 \\ \hline 1 \end{array}$$

You can check your work by multiplying, then adding the remainder.

$$\begin{array}{r} 89\ R1 \\ 3\overline{)\mathbf{268}} \\ 240 \\ \hline 28 \\ -27 \\ \hline 1 \end{array} \qquad \begin{array}{r} 89 \\ \times\ 3 \\ \hline 267 \\ +\ 1 \\ \hline \mathbf{268} \end{array}$$

The answer is right.

1   Check each of these answers.

(a) $\begin{array}{r} 39\ R2 \\ 4\overline{)158} \end{array}$ (b) $\begin{array}{r} 50\ R1 \\ 5\overline{)261} \end{array}$ (c) $\begin{array}{r} 57\ R2 \\ 3\overline{)174} \end{array}$ (d) $\begin{array}{r} 57\ R1 \\ 4\overline{)229} \end{array}$

(e) $\begin{array}{r} 6\ R1 \\ 6\overline{)361} \end{array}$ (f) $\begin{array}{r} 53\ R3 \\ 5\overline{)278} \end{array}$ (g) $\begin{array}{r} 86 \\ 3\overline{)258} \end{array}$ (h) $\begin{array}{r} 45\ R1 \\ 5\overline{)227} \end{array}$

Check your answers!

2   (a) $6\overline{)312}$ (b) $4\overline{)407}$ (c) $3\overline{)148}$

(d) $4\overline{)349}$ (e) $5\overline{)409}$ (f) $8\overline{)839}$

3   (a) $951 \div 8$ (b) $731 \div 3$ (c) $557 \div 3$

(d) $969 \div 5$ (e) $624 \div 6$ (f) $837 \div 7$

Some number investigations.

Leonard misbehaved and was given a lot of boring questions to answer as a punishment. One of them was to add all the numbers from 1 to 100. He worked out the answers in less than a minute.

First he wrote down the numbers 1 to 100 then he reversed them.

1	2	3	4	5	6	98	99	100
100	99	98	97	96	95	3	2	1
101	101	101	101	101	101	101	101	101

He then added.
There were 100 lots of 101, which have a total of 10 100.
But he only needed half of this total, since the numbers were written twice:

10 000 ÷ 2 = 5050

Leonard grew up to become one of the most famous mathematicians the world has known – Leonard Euler: born 1707, died 1783.

1 (a) Use Euler's method to add the numbers 1 to 12.

   (b) Check your answer by making six pairs, each with a sum of 13.

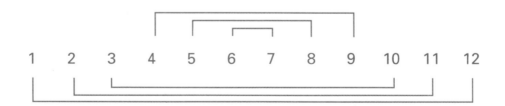

2 Use one of the methods in question 1 to find the sum of:

   (a) the 16 even numbers starting with 2 and ending with 32

   (b) 8, 19, 30, 41, 52, 63 and 74

3 Use a calculator to check your answers to questions 1 and 2.

Street numbers.

Here are the house numbers on the two sides of a street:

1	3	5	7	9	11	13	15	17	19
2	4	6	8	10	12	14	16	18	20

1 What do you notice about all the numbers

   (a) in the top row?   (b) in the bottom row?

2 What is the total of

   (a) the numbers in the top row?

   (b) the numbers in the bottom row?

   (c) all the numbers?

3 Is your answer to 2(b) 10 more than your answer to 2(a)?
   Why should this be expected from looking at the two rows?

4 Take four numbers that are next to each other like this

   7   9   Multiply across as shown.
   8   10 $7 \times 10 = 70$ $9 \times 8 = 72$
   The products, 70 and 72, differ by 2.

   Work with a friend and check this is true for all nine sets of numbers that
   are next to each other. (You may use a calculator).

5 Adding opposite pairs of numbers, we get 3, 7, 11, 15 and so on.

   (a) Why do these increase by 4 each time?

   (b) Why are they all odd numbers?

6 Find out some more things about the street numbers.

The four operations with brackets (2).

$242 + (756 \div 4)$

Work out the numbers in the brackets first.

The answer is 431.

$$4\overline{)756}$$
$$-400$$
$$\overline{356}$$
$$-320$$
$$\overline{36} \quad 242$$
$$-36 \quad +189$$
$$\overline{0} \quad \overline{431}$$

189

1   Work these out.

(a) $(252 \div 2) - 28$ (b) $681 + (396 \div 3)$ (c) $753 - (400 \div 4)$

(d) $(385 \div 5) - 19$ (e) $(462 \div 3) \times 4$ (f) $(507 - 287) \div 5$

(g) $(246 \times 7) \div 7$ (h) $(836 + 259) - 259$ (i) $(444 \div 4) \times 4$

There are different ways for finding the answers to questions (g), (h) and (i). Can you find them?

2   Copy and write $<$, $>$ or $=$ in the circles.

(a) $382 + 167$ ⬤ 275×2 (b) $974 - 395$ ⬤ $504 \div 8$

(c) 68×4 ⬤ $156 \div 6$ (d) 143×6 ⬤ $991 - 143$

(e) 59×46 ⬤ 48×55 (f) $900 - 134$ ⬤ $(378 \div 9) + 737$

3   Make up a story.

NUMBER NEWS $6 \times (3+4) =$

The Greatest Quotient Game.

Which quotient is greater?

1 2)4 5 8   4)8 2 5

2 6)5 8 7   8)7 6 5

3 4)7 8 5   5)8 4 7

4 6)8 3 6   8)6 6 3

Play the game.

A This game is for two or more players.
   Prepare two sets of ten cards with a different digit on each
   (0, 1, 2, 3, 4, 5, 6, 7, 8, 9). Mix up the cards.

B Choose a leader.

C Each player draws a table
   like the following:

D Without looking, the leader picks a card.
   Each player writes the digit in any box in his or her table.

E Repeat D until all four boxes are filled.

F Divide. The player who builds the greatest answer or 'quotient' wins
   the game.

Division puzzles.

Using four different digits you can make up twenty-four different divisions with three digits divided by one digit. Here are some using the digits 4, 8, 6 and 5.

5)486   5)648   6)845   8)654

In all the following questions use the digits 4, 8, 6 and 5.

1   Which of the twenty-four divisions will give:
    (a)   the greatest answer?
    (b)   the smallest answer?
    What are these two answers?
    (You **don't** need to do all twenty-four divisions!)

2   (a)   In how many of the divisions are you dividing by 5?
    (b)   Are there any of these where the division is exact?
    (Exact division means there will not be a remainder.)

3   Find two divisions in which you divide by 4 and there is no remainder.

4   Can you find a division in which you divide by 5 and there is a remainder of 1?

5   Can you find a division in which you divide by 6 and there is a remainder of 2?

Money problems and shopping.

All the record shops in town are having a sale!

1. Judy bought 2 records.
   They cost £3.87 each.
   How much did she pay?

2. Mandy had £8.72. She spent
   £3.79 on a record. How much
   money did she have left?

3. Tony bought 2 records for
   £2.85 each. He gave the
   shop assistant a £10.00 note.
   How much change did he receive?

4. Tom bought 3 records all costing
   the same amount.
   He spent £9.78 altogether?
   What was the cost of each record?

5. Frank bought 3 records for
   £4.35 each.
   What was the total cost?

6. Five records cost £2.90, £5.60,
   £4.30, £3.70 and £4.15.
   What was their average cost?

7. Ann bought 4 records that cost
   £2.85, £3.74, £2.94 and £4.35.
   What was the average cost of
   each record?

8. The average cost of three records
   was £3.60. One cost £4.00 and
   another cost £3.20.
   What was the cost of the other
   record?

Find the number.

9. The number is between 20 and 50.
   If you divide it by 6, you get a
   remainder of 3. If you divide it by
   8, you get a remainder of 7.

10. The number is between 30 and 55.
    If you divide it by 3, you get a
    remainder of 2. If you divide it by
    7, you get a remainder of 1.

Money problems and shopping.

We often have to work out problems when we go shopping.

If we buy three tins, how much does each one cost?

To find the cost of 1 tin, we can divide:

$$
\begin{array}{r}
26 \\
3\overline{)79} \\
-60 \\
\hline
19 \\
-18 \\
\hline
1
\end{array}
$$

Since there is a remainder, we know that the cost of 1 tin is between 26p and 27p. Follow the rule of rounding **up** to the next penny. Is this the same as rounding to the nearest penny?

1   How much does each jar cost?

2   What is the cost of 1 grapefruit?

3   What is the cost of each melon?

Strawberries
2 boxes for £1.19

4 What will be the cost of 3 boxes?

Hint: Add the costs of 2 boxes and 1 box.

5 If 2 boxes of mushrooms cost £1.89, what is the cost of 1 box?

6 If jelly costs 79p for 4 packets, how much will 5 packets cost?

7 Orange juice costs £1.17 for 3 cartons. Terry buys 3 cartons, one for himself and one each for two friends. How much should he charge each friend?
Each friend has only a £1 coin, how much change should he give to each of them?

8 Bread is on special offer: 4 loaves for £1.59. Derek buys a carton of milk for 22p and 5 loaves of bread. What is the total cost?

9 Jam is on special offer:
3 jars of apricot for £1.06 and 4 jars of strawberry for £1.81.
What is the cost of 4 jars of apricot jam and 5 jars of strawberry jam?

10 Find some special offers from a shop. Make up some problems for a friend to solve. Your friend can make up some problems for you to solve.

1	46 × 8	2	57 × 6
3	86 × 5	4	93 × 4
5	78 × 3	6	92 × 9
7	66 × 2	8	39 × 7
9	45 × 1	10	89 × 0
11	64 × 7	12	17 × 8
13	5 × 9	14	32 × 6

STAGE 11   **Money problems and shopping.**   **25**

BASIC programs.

You have met this BASIC program for producing multiples of a number, in this case 5. This prints on the screen 5, 10, 15, 20, . . . , 50.

But how can you use the computer to test if a number is a multiple of 3 or 5 or 7?

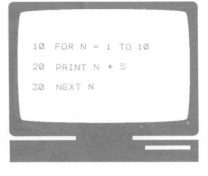

```
10  FOR N = 1 TO 10
20  PRINT N * 5
30  NEXT N
```

1 Divide each of these numbers by 5:

15   6   9   20   10   18   25

What do you notice about the results if the number is a multiple of 5?
What do you notice about the results if the number is **not** a multiple of 5?
Those which are multiples of 5 give a whole number (or integer) as a result.
There is a BASIC instruction INT. See what happens when you type in:

PRINT INT (3.5)	PRINT INT (6)	PRINT INT (4.8)
PRINT INT (3)	PRINT INT (5.3)	PRINT INT (5)

2 Copy and complete this:

15/5 =   INT (15/5) =
18/5 =   INT (18/5) =
10/5 =   INT (10/5) =
13/5 =   INT (13/5) =
22/5 =   INT (22/5) =
25/5 =   INT (25/5) =

If a number n is a multiple of 5
then n/5 = INT (n/5)

This BASIC program will test for multiples:

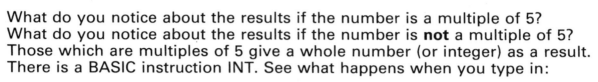

```
10  INPUT X
20  IF X/7 = INT(X/7) THEN
    PRINT "YES"
30  IF X/7 <> INT(X/7) THEN
    PRINT "NO"
```

At line 10 you type in a number to be tested.
Line 20 tests to see if it is a multiple of 7.
Line 30 tests to see if it is not equal (<>) to a multiple of 7.

3 Use your program to find out which of these are multiples of 7:

45   91   112   146   173   203   234   364

4 Change lines 20 and 30 so that you test for multiples of 9, of 13, of 17.
Which of the following are multiples of 9, 13 or 17?

104   135   126   102   221   117

5 Write a BASIC program that will test all numbers from 1 to 100 and print out those which are multiples of 7.
Change line 10 so that X is given values of 1 to 100.
Change line 20 so that the number (X) is printed rather than yes.
Line 30 is not needed.
Add line 40 so that the next value of X is called up.

Inverses.

A	B	C
378	1345	1345
+ 967	− 967	− 378
1345	378	967

967
+ 378
1345

Notice the connection between addition and subtraction.
If you add the lower two numbers in the subtractions B and C you get the top number.

Addition is the **inverse** of subtraction.
Subtraction is the **inverse** of addition.

Inverses cancel each other.
For example, if you add 97 to any number and then subtract 97, you will get the number that you started with.
Thus 349 + 97 − 97 = 349, since 97 − 97 = 0.

1   Do these subtractions then check your answers by addition.

(a)   1381   (b)   2006   (c)   9162   (d)   21000   (e)   43 762
  − 743   − 314   − 977   − 6835   − 29 907

2   Write down any number. Multiply it by 7.
Divide the result by 7. You should be left with the number that you started with.

(a)   Try with other numbers first multiplied and then divided by 7.

(b)   Try with other numbers first multiplied and then divided by 9.

You are always left with your starting number no matter what number you first multiply and then divide by.

Multiplication is the **inverse** of division.
Division is the **inverse** of multiplication.

3   Do these divisions, then check your answers by multiplication.

(a)   117 ÷ 9   (b) 936 ÷ 12   (c) 1125 ÷ 25   (d) 3294 ÷ 54

Multiplying by multiples of ten.

How would you find the total number of bulbs?

Here is how Jean found the number of bulbs.

Jean

12 in each box
×3
36 in each stack

36 in each stack
×10 stacks
360 light bulbs

$$\begin{array}{r} 12 \\ \times 30 \\ \hline 360 \end{array}$$

12 bulbs in each box
×30 boxes of bulbs
360

To find this product, Jean first multiplied 12 by 3.

Then she multiplied that answer by 10.

1 **Multiply.**

(a) $\begin{array}{r} 42 \\ \times 20 \end{array}$ *Multiply by 2 and then by 10.*

(b) $\begin{array}{r} 31 \\ \times 30 \end{array}$ *Multiply by 3 and then by 10.*

(c) $\begin{array}{r} 43 \\ \times 20 \end{array}$ *Multiply by 2 and then by 10.*

(d) $\begin{array}{r} 16 \\ \times 40 \end{array}$ *Multiply by 4 and then by 10.*

You can write
the 0 first
and then
multiply by 4.

53
× 40
————
2120

2   Multiply. Write the 0 first.

(a)   34   (b)   36   (c)   30   (d)   23   (e)   48
    × 20   × 20   × 30   × 40   × 50

(f)   46   (g)   68   (h)   93   (i)   82   (j)   84
    × 40   × 50   × 60   × 70   × 50

(k)   43   (l)   84   (m)   79   (n)   42   (o)   95
    × 80   × 80   × 70   × 90   × 90

(p)   318   (q)   284   (r)   358   (s)   472   (t)   529
    × 20   × 30   × 40   × 30   × 50

---

3    How much will 20 stamps cost?

4   How many biscuits in 30 boxes?

5   Mark earns £4.50 each week. How much will he earn in 40 weeks?

6   Gemma earns £1.25 an hour for baby-sitting.
    One month she baby-sat for 5 hours each Saturday.
    There were 4 Saturdays in the month. How much did she earn?

Multiplying by a two-digit number.

There are 24 sardines in each can.
There are 23 cans.
The total number of sardines is

```
   24
 ×23
```

Here is how to find the product.

Step 1. Multiply by 20.

```
   24
 ×23
 480  (24 × 20)
```

Step 2. Multiply by 3.

```
   24
 ×23
 480  (24 × 20)
  72  (24 × 3)
```

Step 3. Add.

```
   24
 ×23
 480  (24 × 20)
  72  (24 × 3)
 552  (24 × 23)
```

1   Copy and complete:

(a)
```
    42
  ×23
  840  (42 × 20)
  126  (42 × 3)
 ____  (42 × 23)
```

(b)
```
    43
  ×32
 1290  (43 × 30)
   86  (43 × 2)
 ____  (43 × 32)
```

(c)
```
    32
  ×26
  640  (32 × 20)
 ____  (32 × 6)
 ____  (32 × 26)
```

(d)
```
    54
  ×43
 2160  (54 × 40)
 ____  (54 × 3)
```

(e)
```
    78
  ×53
 3650  (78 × 50)
 ____  (78 × 3)
```

(f)
```
    65
  ×48
 2600  (65 × 40)
 ____  (65 × 8)
```

(g)
```
    53
  ×49
 2120  (53 × 40)
 ____  (53 × 9)
```

(h)
```
    49
  ×53
 2450  (49 × 50)
 ____  (49 × 3)
```

(i)
```
    54
  ×32
 1620  (54 × 30)
 ____  (54 × 2)
```

2 (a) 87   (b) 58   (c) 79   (d) 65   (e) 80
       × 47   × 42   × 19   × 25   × 52

   (f) 74   (g) 93   (h) 76   (i) 85   (j) 96
       × 29   × 50   × 43   × 74   × 44

   (k) 54p   (l) 63p   (m) 69p   (n) 77p   (o) 86p
       × 63   × 63   × 41   × 55   × 48

   (p) 52p   (q) 78p   (r) 65p   (s) 79p   (t) 95p
       × 37   × 58   × 49   × 27   × 63

3   28 days.
    How many hours?

4   49 tins of beans cost 25p each.
    What is the total cost?

5   26 comics cost 17p each.
    What is the total cost?

6   54 buses.
    23 people in each bus.
    How many people?

Copy and complete:

7

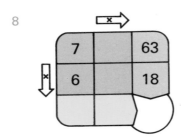

8	3	
5	7	

8

7		63
6		18

9

8		72
		35
	45	

Rounding and multiplication.

We can estimate by first rounding to the nearest 10, then multiplying.

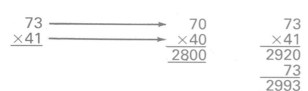

$$\begin{array}{r} 89 \\ \times 52 \\ \hline \end{array}$$

Round to the nearest 10

Round to the nearest 10

$$\begin{array}{r} 90 \\ \times 50 \\ \hline 4500 \end{array}$$

$$\begin{array}{r} 89 \\ \times 52 \\ \hline 4450 \\ 178 \\ \hline 4628 \end{array}$$ The answer is close to the estimate.

$$\begin{array}{r} 73 \\ \times 41 \end{array} \longrightarrow \begin{array}{r} 70 \\ \times 40 \\ \hline 2800 \end{array}$$

$$\begin{array}{r} 73 \\ \times 41 \\ \hline 2920 \\ 73 \\ \hline 2993 \end{array}$$ The answer is close to the estimate.

Estimate by rounding to the nearest 10 and then multiply.
Check your answer with your estimate.

1 $\begin{array}{r} 82 \\ \times 36 \\ \hline \end{array}$
2 $\begin{array}{r} 59 \\ \times 54 \\ \hline \end{array}$
3 $\begin{array}{r} 93 \\ \times 27 \\ \hline \end{array}$
4 $\begin{array}{r} 48 \\ \times 12 \\ \hline \end{array}$
5 $\begin{array}{r} 76 \\ \times 31 \\ \hline \end{array}$

6 $\begin{array}{r} 42 \\ \times 69 \\ \hline \end{array}$
7 $\begin{array}{r} 92 \\ \times 52 \\ \hline \end{array}$
8 $\begin{array}{r} 73 \\ \times 40 \\ \hline \end{array}$
9 $\begin{array}{r} 78 \\ \times 23 \\ \hline \end{array}$
10 $\begin{array}{r} 65 \\ \times 49 \\ \hline \end{array}$

11 (a) $\begin{array}{r} 72 \\ \times 25 \\ \hline \end{array}$
(b) $\begin{array}{r} 25 \\ \times 72 \\ \hline \end{array}$
12 (a) $\begin{array}{r} 92 \\ \times 38 \\ \hline \end{array}$
(b) $\begin{array}{r} 38 \\ \times 92 \\ \hline \end{array}$

13 $\begin{array}{r} 78 \\ \times 29 \\ \hline 1560 \\ 702 \\ \hline 2262 \end{array}$ Without calculating, write down the answer to $\begin{array}{r} 29 \\ \times 78 \\ \hline \end{array}$

14 Use a calculator to check that $96 \times 37 = 37 \times 96$.
Check other pairs of numbers in the same way.

Investigating products.

Look at this multiplication square for up to 10 × 10.

×	0	1	2	3	4	5	6	7	8	9	10
0	0	0	0	0	0	0	0	0	0	0	0
1	0	1	2	3	4	5	6	7	8	9	10
2	0	2	4	6	8	10	12	14	16	18	20
3	0	3	6	9	12	15	18	21	24	27	30
4	0	4	8	12	16	20	24	28	32	36	40
5	0	5	10	15	20	25	30	35	40	45	50
6	0	6	12	18	24	30	36	42	48	54	60
7	0	7	14	21	28	35	42	49	56	63	70
8	0	8	16	24	32	40	48	56	64	72	80
9	0	9	18	27	36	45	54	63	72	81	90
10	0	10	20	30	40	50	60	70	80	90	100

Here are four numbers in a square that can be taken from the large square.

20	24
25	30

Multiply the numbers in the opposite corners.
20 × 30 = 600
25 × 24 = 600 The products are equal.

1   See if the products are equal for these squares.

(a)

48	54
56	63

(b)

72	81
80	90

(c)

32	36
40	45

2   Find the missing numbers from these squares, then see if the products are equal.

(a)

15	
	24

(b)

42	
49	

(c)

64	

3   Investigate what happens when you use a 3 by 3 square and multiply the numbers in the opposite corners as before.
For example: Does 21 × 45 = 27 × 35?

21	24	27
28	32	36
35	40	45

Try larger squares and look for the same property.

Shapes and angles.

Tim tore the corners off a rectangle.
They fitted together without any gaps.
The angles meeting at a point without
any gaps added up to 360°.
The angles of Tim's rectangle added
up to 360°.

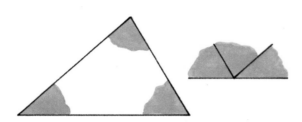

Maggie tore the corners off a triangle.
They fitted together to give
a straight line.
A straight line gives an angle of 180°.
The angles of Maggie's triangle added
up to 180°.

1   What is the sum of the angles of a square?
    Draw a square. Tear off the corners.
    Fit them together to check your answer.

2   (a) Trace this **quadrilateral** (four-sided figure).
         Cut it out and tear off the corners.
    (b) Do they fit together without any gaps?
    (c) What is the sum of the angles of the
         quadrilateral?

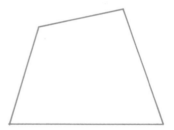

    Repeat question 2 with these quadrilaterals.

3

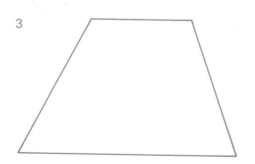

4

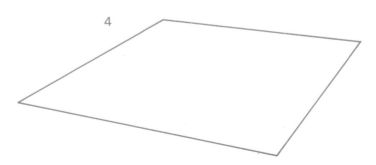

5 (a) Trace this triangle.
       Cut it out and tear off the corners. Fit them together.
   (b) Do they form a straight line?
   (c) What is the sum of the angles of the triangle?

Repeat question 5 with these triangles.

6

7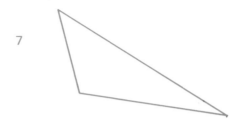

You should find that the angles of every quadrilateral fit together without gaps.
The sum of the angles of a quadrilateral is 360°.

The angles of every triangle fit together to make a straight line.
The sum of the angles of a triangle is 180°.

8 Use a protractor to measure the
   angles of these quadrilaterals.
   Copy the table and record
   your results on it.

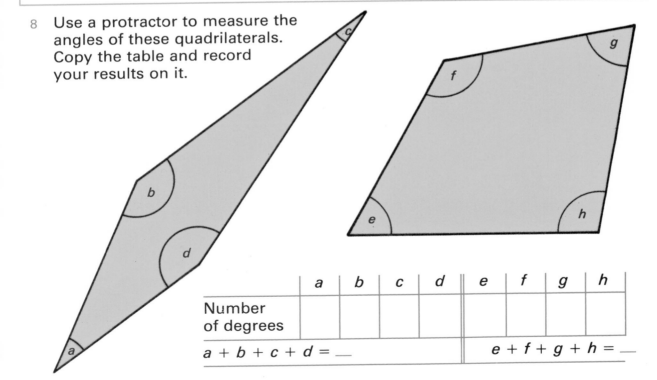

	a	b	c	d	e	f	g	h
Number of degrees								

$a + b + c + d =$ __ $e + f + g + h =$ __

Angles of a triangle.

From your work on pages 34 and 35 you would expect the angles of a triangle to add up to 180°. Check that this is true for all the triangles below.

Copy the table below.

Triangle	1	2	3
a			
b			
c			
a + b + c			

Measure the angles. Record them on the table. When you have finished measuring, find the sums.

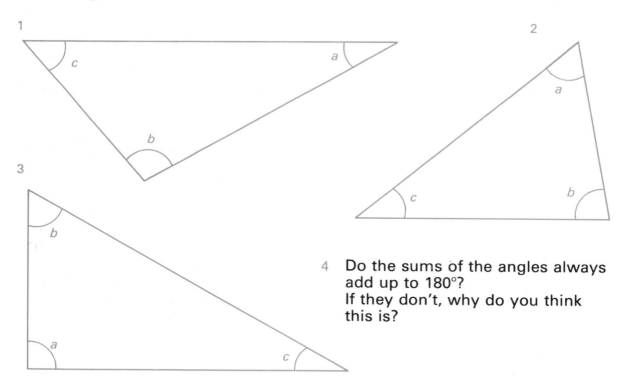

4   Do the sums of the angles always add up to 180°?
If they don't, why do you think this is?

⑤   Draw some triangles of your own. Find the sum of the angles. Discuss your answers with your teacher.

Scale drawings.

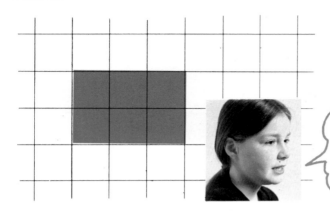

The squares have sides of 1 cm.
Carol has drawn a plan
of her garden.
1 cm represents 10 m, or 1000 cm.
This is written like this 1:1000.

The length of my garden is 30 metres.
This is 3 centimetres on my plan.
The width of my garden is 20 metres.
This is 2 centimetres on my plan.

Use Carol's scale.

1   What would these lengths on the
    plan represent?
    (a) **4 cm**   (b) **6 cm**   (c) **10 cm**
    (d) **15 cm**   (e) **½ cm**   (f) **0.8 cm**

2   What lengths on the plan would
    represent these measurements?
    (a) **50 m**   (b) **70 m**   (c) **100 m**
    (d) **6 m**   (e) **12 m**   (f) **37 m**

3   (a) What is the perimeter of the
        rectangle on Carol's plan?
    (b) What is the perimeter of
        Carol's garden?

4   Use centimetre-squared paper.
    The scale is 1:1000.
    (a) Draw the plan of a lawn which
        is rectangular and has sides of
        25 metres and 10 metres.
    (b) What is the perimeter of the
        rectangle you have drawn?
    (c) What is the perimeter of the
        lawn?

5   The scale on this map is
    1 cm to 5 km.
    (a) Measure Arden to Buckthorn,
        in centimetres.
    (b) What is the distance between
        Arden and Buckthorn in
        kilometres?

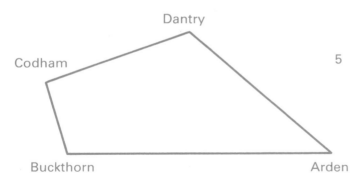

6   Copy and complete this table.

	Arden to Buckthorn	Buckthorn to Codham	Codham to Dantry	Dantry to Arden
Distance in centimetres on the map				
Distance in kilometres that is represented				

Scale drawings.

This rocket is drawn to a scale of 1 cm to 2 m.

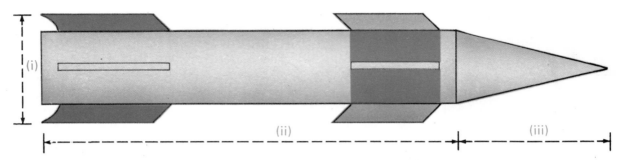

1   Copy and complete these tables.
    Insert the equivalent metres in (a) and the equivalent centimetres in (b).

(a)

Scaled length	1.0 cm	1.5 cm	2.0 cm	2.5 cm	3.0 cm	3.5 cm	4.0 cm	4.5 cm
True length	2 m							

(b)

Scaled length								
True length	10 m	14 m	15 m	20 m	24 m	27 m	30 m	40 m

2   (a) Measure in centimetres the following parts of the rocket shown at the
        top of the page.
        (i) width   (ii) length of main body   (iii) length of nose
    (b) What are the true measurements?

3   This aeroplane is drawn to a scale of 1:600.

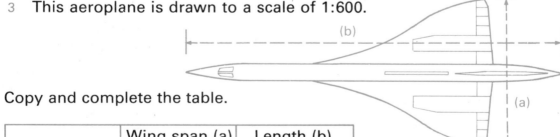

Copy and complete the table.

	Wing span (a)	Length (b)
Scaled length		
True length		

Surveying.

Land surveyors determine the shape and size of a part of the Earth's surface. They also set boundaries for property.

Surveyors use an instrument called a theodolite for sighting in a 'straight line' and for determining horizontal and vertical angles. Distances are found by measuring with a surveyor's tape. While a survey is being made, surveyors generally record the data in a field book.

Here are two plots from a field book. Make a scale drawing of each plot. Use a protractor to draw the 'corner' angles.

Use as large a scale as possible to reduce errors.

1

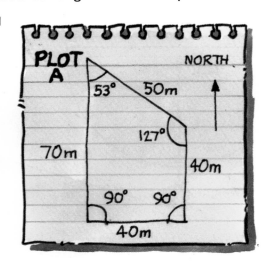

2

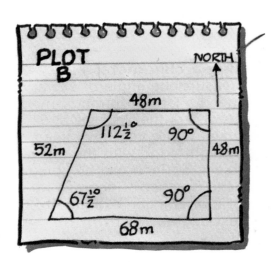

3   Discuss with your teacher how to survey part or all of your school grounds.

Finding heights and distances.

Find the height of a tree.

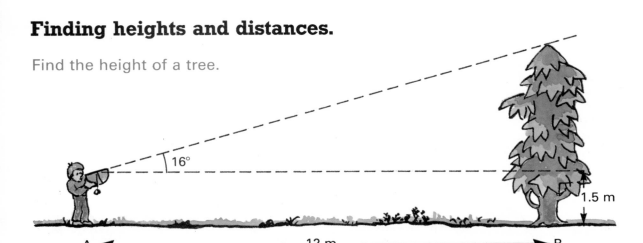

A ← 12 m → B

The **angle of elevation** is 16°. It is measured **upwards** from the horizontal. By measuring the distance AB and making a scale drawing, the height of the tree can be found.

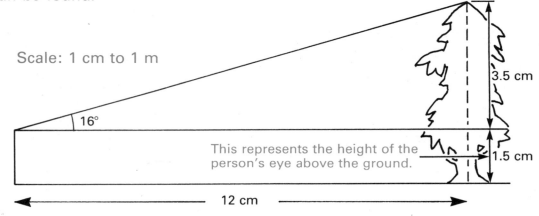

Scale: 1 cm to 1 m

16°

3.5 cm

This represents the height of the person's eye above the ground. 1.5 cm

12 cm

The total height of the tree is 5 cm on the plan so it is actually 5 m high.

Making a clinometer.

To measure the angle of elevation you need a large protractor made of card. Mark the degrees at 5° intervals. When you have lined up the straight edge with the top of an object, a friend will be able to read the number of degrees for you. He or she can estimate to the nearest degree.

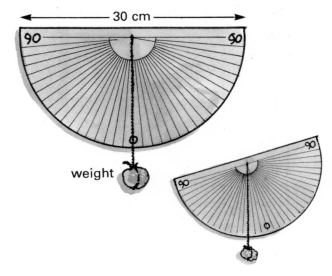

30 cm

90   90

weight

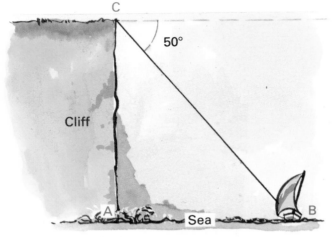

C

50°

Cliff

A

Sea

B

The **angle of depression** is 50°.
It is measured **downwards** from the horizontal.

1 Take the height of the cliff as 70 metres.
Make a scale drawing and find the distance of the boat from the bottom of the cliff.
(*Hint:* ∠ ACB = 90° − 50° = 40°)

2 An aeroplane flies due north for a distance of 120km.
It then changes course and flies 200 km due east.

(a) Make a scale drawing and find the distance from its starting point.

(b) The angle of elevation of the aeroplane after it had travelled 60 km is measured by an observer at the starting point. The angle is 12°.
Make a scale drawing and find the height of the aeroplane.

3 Use the methods on page 40 to find the height of some trees, buildings, telegraph poles and so on.

keeping skills sharp

A

B

C

The clocks show times in the afternoon.
1 Write down the 24-hour clock times.
2 What is the difference in time between A and C?

Speed.

Tina went jogging.
When she was tired she walked.
She covered 10 miles in 2 hours.
Her average speed was 10 miles
divided by 2 hours, which is
5 miles per hour (5 mph).

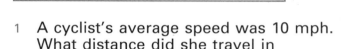

Average speed = $\dfrac{\text{Total distance}}{\text{Total time}}$

1   A cyclist's average speed was 10 mph.
What distance did she travel in

(a)   3 hours?   (b) $\frac{1}{2}$ hour?   (c) $1\frac{1}{2}$ hours?   (d) $4\frac{1}{2}$ hours?

2   What is the average speed for these distances and times?

(a)   58 miles in 2 hours?   (b) 72 miles in 6 hours?   (c) 87 miles in 4 hours?

3   How long would it take to travel 150 miles at an average speed of:

(a)   10 mph?   (b) 5 mph?   (c) 30 mph?

4

Mike travelled 12 miles by bus,
taking 1 hour.
He then walked 6 miles in the next
two hours. Find:

(a)   the total distance travelled

(b)   the total time taken

(c)   the average speed for the whole
journey.

5   A salesman drove for 40 km at an average speed of 80 km/h. He then drove
a further 135 km at an average speed of 90 km/h. Find:

(a)   the total distance travelled   (b) the total time taken

(c)   the average speed for the whole journey.

Length and distance.

Remember   1 cm = 10 mm   1 m = 100 cm = 1000 mm   1 km = 1000 m

Examples

48 mm = 4 cm 8 mm = 4.8 cm   6.72 m = 6 m 72 cm = 672 cm

1   Change these to millimetres.

(a) 7 cm   (b) 3.5 cm   (c) 2.1 cm   (d) 5.36 cm

2   Change these to centimetres.

(a) 60 mm   (b) 83 mm   (c) 790 mm   (d) 14.6 mm

3   Change these to the units given in brackets.

(a) 80 cm (m)   (b) 4.3 m (cm)   (c) 9.12 m (cm)

(d) 7900 cm (m)   (e) 1.82 cm (mm)   (f) 4560 mm (cm)

Now try using what you know about length.

4   Together with a friend,
choose a small object, such as a watch.
Challenge your friend to estimate the
length in mm, while you estimate it in cm.
Write down your estimates.
Measure to check the length of the object,
then compare and discuss your estimates.

Do this with several small things.
Do you get better with practice?

5   Do this with a friend.
You will need a local Ordnance Survey map.

Choose somewhere local, near the school, that you both know.
Together, agree on an estimate of the distance **in km** by road from your
chosen place to your school.

Now measure the distance on the map. (A piece of string will help you to
measure round bends in the road.) Work out the distance this represents.

How good was your estimate?

Distances in km.

	Aberdeen	Birmingham	Brighton	Cardiff	Exeter	London	Newcastle
Aberdeen		680	956	843	927	861	380
Birmingham	680		285	171	253	190	344
Brighton	956	285		296	277	85	550
Cardiff	843	171	296		187	246	515
Exeter	927	253	277	187		277	595
London	861	190	85	246	277		450
Newcastle	380	344	550	515	595	450	

1 (a) Reading along the first row, the distance
from Aberdeen to Cardiff is 843 km.
What is the distance from Cardiff to Aberdeen?
   (b) What is the distance from:
     (i) Brighton to Newcastle — is it the same as Newcastle to Brighton?
     (ii) Exeter to London — is it the same as London to Exeter?
     (iii) Birmingham to Cardiff — is it the same as Cardiff to Birmingham?

2 Write down these distances:
   (a) London to Aberdeen   (b) Exeter to Newcastle
   (c) Birmingham to Brighton (d) Cardiff to Brighton

3 A traveller lives in London.
He drove to Birmingham and then to Newcastle.
How far did he travel?

4 A lady living in Aberdeen drove to Newcastle and then to Cardiff.
She returned to Aberdeen by the same route.
   (a) What distance did she drive from Aberdeen to Cardiff?
   (b) What was the total distance she travelled?

5 Which is nearer to Birmingham and by how many kilometres?
   (a) Newcastle or Exeter?   (b) London or Aberdeen?

6 Penny cycled from London to Birmingham in 10 hours.
   (a) What was her average speed?
   (b) How far would she have travelled from London in 3 hours at the
       average speed?
   (c) How far from Birmingham would she then be?

7 Mike drove from Cardiff to Brighton.
   He travelled the first 2 hours at an average speed
   of 100 km/h, then stopped for 1 hour.
   (a) How far from Brighton was he when he stopped?
   (b) Mike was held up by heavy traffic for the rest of the journey. His
       average speed was only 48 km/h.
       How long did he take to complete the journey?
   (c) How long did it take Mike to travel from Cardiff to Brighton altogether?

8 A coach tour started in Birmingham and went to London, then to Brighton,
   Exeter, Cardiff and back to Birmingham.
   The total driving time was 13 hours.
   (a) What was the total distance?
   (b) What was the average speed?

9 Calculate the average speed for each of these journeys.
   (a) Aberdeen, Birmingham, Newcastle and back to Aberdeen in 26 hours.
   (b) Brighton, London, Birmingham and back to Brighton in 14 hours.

10 You need a chart showing distances between main towns in kilometres.
   (a) Find out how to read the distances on the chart.
   (b) Which of the towns on the chart is nearest to where you live?
   (c) Find the distance from that town to:
       (i) London   (ii) Cardiff   (iii) Edinburgh   (iv) Liverpool

Mastermind with numbers.

This game is for two players.

One player writes down a four-digit number. The other player has to find out what the number is. Keep a record of all the guesses made.

This is the beginning of a game played by Sarah and Tom.

Sarah has written down her number: 8612

Tom's first guess is seven thousand, nine hundred and sixty-one.

Sarah says: 'Two digits are correct. No digits are in the correct position.'

(Note 1 and 6 are the correct digits but Tom is not told which ones are correct.)

Tom: 'Eight thousand, one hundred and fifty-three'

Sarah: 'Two digits are correct. One digit is in the correct position.'

Tom: 'Eight thousand, four hundred and twenty-six.'

Sarah: 'Three digits are correct. One digit is in the correct position.'

The game continues like this until Tom has found Sarah's number.

1 (a) **Play the game with a friend. Let your friend be the first players and write down the number. Count the number of 'guesses' you make before you find the number.**

   (b) **Now you choose the number and let your friend find out what it is.**

   The player who makes the smaller number of guesses wins.

2 Continue the game so that each player has at least four turns at finding the number.

3 Play the game with five-digit numbers.

1 Copy the table below. Complete it by writing YES or NO in each box.

	Monkey	Duck	Crocodile	Bat	Fish	Beaver
Swim						
Fly						
Fur						
Feathers						

2 (a) Which animals cannot swim and do not have feathers?

(b) Which animals do not have fur but can swim?

(c) Which animals have fur but cannot fly?

3 Make up questions (like those in question 2) which have these answers:

(a) bat   (b) fish, beaver and crocodile   (c) duck

4 Name one animal for each of the conditions (a), (b) and (c) below.
None of these animals are any of the ones pictured above.

(a) Has feathers but no fur, and cannot fly or swim.

(b) Has fur but no feathers, and cannot fly or swim.

(c) Has neither fur nor feathers, and cannot fly or swim.

Find the robber.

Sixteen people were suspected of various robberies.

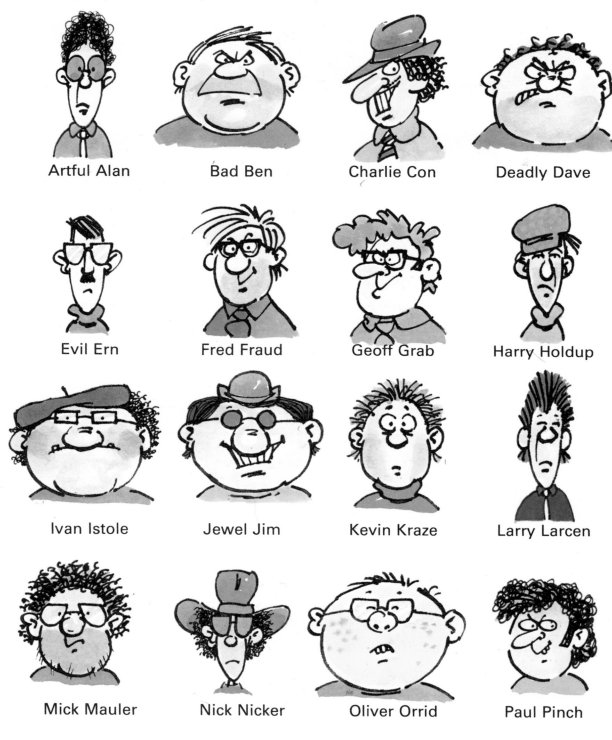

Artful Alan Bad Ben Charlie Con Deadly Dave

Evil Ern Fred Fraud Geoff Grab Harry Holdup

Ivan Istole Jewel Jim Kevin Kraze Larry Larcen

Mick Mauler Nick Nicker Oliver Orrid Paul Pinch

Use initials to write your answers.
For example, write A.A. instead of Artful Alan.

1   List the possible suspects if the robber:
    (a) has straight hair, wears glasses but no tie;
    (b) has curly hair, is thin and wears a hat but no tie.

2   Copy and complete this table for all suspects.

	Curly hair	Wears glasses	Thin/medium/fat	Wears a tie	Wears a hat
A.A.	Yes	Yes	Thin	Yes	No
B.B.					

3   The first witness said the robber was thin and wore glasses. The second
    witness said the robber was thin and wore a hat.
    Sergeant Coppem drew this diagram.

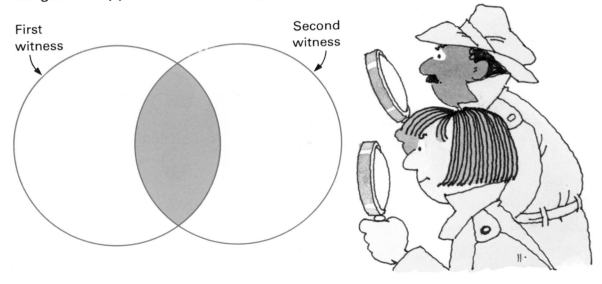

First witness   Second witness

Copy the diagram.
Complete it by writing the initials of the possible suspects in each loop.
The shaded part is for suspects which fit the descriptions of both witnesses.
Who committed the crime?

4   One witness said the robber he saw was fat, wore glasses but was not
    wearing a hat.
    (a) If the witness was correct in all aspects, who could have been the
        robber?
    (b) If the witness was mistaken about one fact, but correct about all the
        others, who could have been the robber?
        If there is more than one suspect, list them all.

Multiples, common multiples and LCM.

If you multiply 3 by any number, you get a **multiple** of 3.

$3 \times 8 = 24$, so 24 is a multiple of 3.

$3 \times 13 = 39$, so 39 is also a multiple of 3.

Here are the multiples of 3 in ascending order:

3, 6, 9, 12, 15, 18, 21, 24, 27, 30, 33, 36, 39, . . .

The multiples of 4 are:

4, 8, 12, 16, 20, 24, 28, 32, 36, . . .

You can see that 12, 24 and 36 are multiples of 3 and 4.
12, 24 and 36 are **common multiples** of 3 and 4.

12 is the **lowest common multiple** of 3 and 4.
This can be shortened to
12 is the **LCM** of 3 and 4.

1   Write the first eight multiples of (a) 6 and (b) 8.

(c)   Which of the multiples are common to both 6 and 8?

(d)   What is the lowest common multiple of 6 and 8?

2   Find the lowest common multiple of:

(a)   5 and 10   (b)   10 and 15   (c)   15 and 20   (d)   20 and 25

Can you see a pattern in the answers to question 2?
Try to **predict** the answer to the following question, then check whether you were right.

3   What is the lowest common multiple of 25 and 30?

4   Try the same investigation with any sequence of equally spaced numbers you choose. (For example, 3 and 4, 4 and 5, 5 and 6, and so on.) Can you find a pattern in the answers?

Multiple puzzles.

1 Pat wants to add $\frac{3}{4}$ and $\frac{1}{6}$. She decides to change them into equivalent fractions so that the denominators are the same.

  (a) What is the lowest number which is a multiple of both 4 and 6?

  (b) Change $\frac{3}{4}$ and $\frac{1}{6}$ into equivalent fractions with your answer to (a) as denominator.

  (c) Add $\frac{3}{4}$ and $\frac{1}{6}$.

2 Two clocks are broken. One goes 'Bong!' every 9 minutes, and the other goes 'Cuckoo!' every 12 minutes. They go 'Bong! Cuckoo!' together at 10 a.m.

  (a) When will they next go 'Bong! Cuckoo!' together?

  (b) At the fourth 'Bong! Cuckoo!' Dad loses his temper and throws the clocks in the dustbin. At what time are they thrown away?

3 Sue is trying to sleep, but she can hear taps dripping in the bathroom. The hot tap in the basin drips every 10 seconds and the cold tap drips every 8 seconds. She hears a loud plop when both taps drip together. How many seconds will it be before the next loud plop?

4 Disaster strikes. The bath taps start dripping as well. The hot tap drips every 7 seconds and the cold tap every 16 seconds. Sue hears an extra loud 'PLOP!' when all four taps drip together. How many extra loud PLOPS will she hear in the next 10 minutes? (Talk about this with a friend. Use a calculator if you want to!)

Perimeter.

Remember, the perimeter of a shape is the distance around the shape.
Here are some examples.

The sides of a square are 2.8 cm.

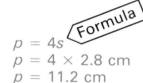

To use this formula to find a perimeter, I write the length of a side of the square as s, and p for the perimeter.

2.8 cm
2.8 cm
2.8 cm
+ 2.8 cm
———
11.2 cm

Formula
$p = 4s$
$p = 4 \times 2.8 \text{ cm}$
$p = 11.2 \text{ cm}$

The perimeter is 11.2 cm.

The sides of a rectangle are 5.6 m and 3.7 m. Find the perimeter.

5.6 m
3.7 m
5.6 m
+ 3.7 m
———
18.6 m

3.7 m

5.6 m

Formula
$p = 2l + 2b$
$p = (2 \times 5.6 \text{ m}) + (2 \times 3.7 \text{ m})$
$p = 11.2 \text{ m} + 7.4 \text{ m}$
$p = 18.6 \text{ m}$

The perimeter is 18.6 m.

---

1 Calculate the perimeter of a square with sides:
   (a) **3 cm**   (b) **4.5 cm**   (c) **3.8 cm**   (d) **4.6 m**

2 Calculate the perimeter of a rectangle with sides:
   (a) **2 cm and 5 cm**   (b) **1.7 cm and 6 cm**   (c) **3.8 and 1.9 cm**

3 Using the formula $p = 4s$ calculate:
   (a) p when s = 6.2 m   (b) p when s = 5.4 m

4 Give the perimeter of each figure.

(a)

3.86 m

2.95 m

(b)

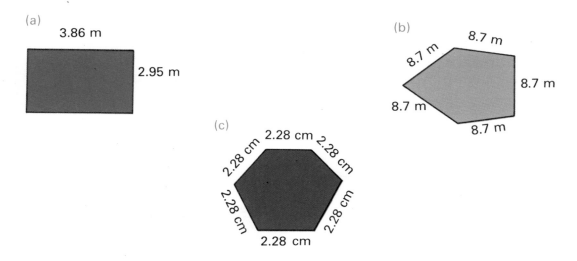

8.7 m
8.7 m
8.7 m
8.7 m
8.7 m

(c)

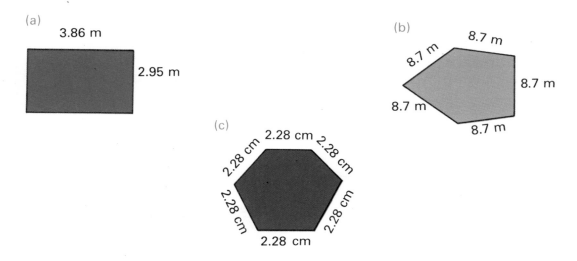

2.28 cm
2.28 cm
2.28 cm
2.28 cm
2.28 cm
2.28 cm

(d)

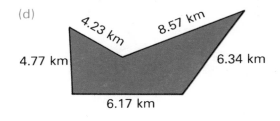

4.23 km
8.57 km
4.77 km
6.34 km
6.17 km

(e)

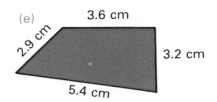

3.6 cm
2.9 cm
3.2 cm
5.4 cm

(f)

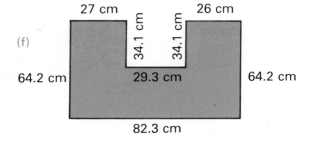

27 cm
34.1 cm
34.1 cm
26 cm
64.2 cm
29.3 cm
64.2 cm
82.3 cm

5 Use the formula $p = 2l + 2b$ to calculate
the perimeter of rectangles with sides:
(a) 4 cm and 5 cm (b) 2.8 m and 4 m (c) 3.6 m and 1.7 m

6 The perimeter of a rectangle is 56 m.
The length of the rectangle is 15 m.
Calculate the breadth of the rectangle.

Multiplying three-digit numbers by two-digit numbers.

174 boxes of soup have been delivered to the supermarket.
There are 24 cans in each box.
You can find the total number of cans by
using the **distributive property** of multiplication.
Instead of multiplying by 24, you multiply by 20 and then by 4.

174 × 24 = (174 × 20) + (174 × 4)

Step 1.   Multiply by 20.

```
  174
× 24
 3480    cans in 20 boxes.
```

Step 2.   Multiply by 4.

```
  174
× 24
 3480
  696    cans in 4 boxes.
```

Step 3.   Add.

```
  174
× 24
 3480
  696
 4176    cans altogether.
```

Another example.

```
   £2.43
×    56
£121.50    (£2.43 × 50)
£ 14.58    (£2.43 ×  6)
£136.08    (£2.43 × 56)
```

1 Give each product.

(a)   153   (b)   237   (c)   173   (d)   395   (e)   460
    × 24   × 25   × 32   × 43   × 38

(f)   149   (g)   283   (h)   354   (i)   278   (j)   495
    × 49   × 45   × 53   × 64   × 58

(k)   158   (l)   296   (m)   342   (n)   506   (o)   821
    × 31   × 45   × 62   × 51   × 78

(p) £1.42   (q) £6.95   (r) £9.24   (s) £5.38   (t) £8.26
    ×   46   ×   70   ×   43   ×   97   ×   64

2

How many apples in 124 boxes?

3

How much will 18 tickets cost?

4 Bill can cycle 207 m in one
   minute. How far can he cycle in
   19 minutes?

5 While on a 4 day car trip,
   Miss Johnson averaged
   61 km an hour.
   How far did she drive if she
   drove for 8 hours each day?

6 A record costs £3.85.
   Find the cost of 57 records.

7 A box contains 150 paper
   clips.
   How many clips in 84 boxes?

What's my number?

8 (a) My number is
       68 greater than
       the product of
       42 and 16.

   (b) My number is 54 less
       than the product
       of 232 and 34.

   (c) My number is the
       answer when 89
       is multiplied by the
       sum of 25 and 37.

Multiplication problems.

1 Two cricketers each scored 889 runs in a year.
What was the total number of runs scored?

2 A batsman averaged 64 runs for each of 19 innings.
What was the total number of runs scored?

3 A stadium has 12 sections.
Each section holds 938 people.
What is the total number the stadium can hold?

4 A ticket to watch a match at Newton
football ground costs £4.75.
What is the cost of:
(a) 10 tickets? (b) 23 tickets? (c) 42 tickets?

5 Season tickets for 21 home games at
Bingham football ground cost £85.
Single tickets for each match cost £4.62.
(a) What is the cost of 21 tickets at £4.62 each?
(b) How much is saved by buying a season ticket?

6 A hot-dog seller at a football match
sold 148 hot-dogs at 36p each.
(a) How much money did she get: (i) in pence?
(ii) in pounds?
(b) How much profit would she make if she
had paid 20p for each hot-dog?
(Profit = amount of money collected minus
amount of money paid out.)

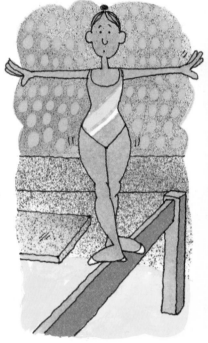

keeping skills sharp

1	2	3	4
426	599	567	8215
3871	1897	382	6936
+ 15968	+ 43625	1496	37435
		+ 3751	+ 12897

5	6	7	8
4367	56342	14030	20030
− 2819	− 38975	− 5862	− 15647

1	2	3	4	5	6	7	8	9	10
11	12	13	14	15	16	17	18	19	20
21	22	23	24	25	26	27	28	29	30
31	32	33	34	35	36	37	38	39	40
41	42	43	44	45	46	47	48	49	50
51	52	53	54	55	56	57	58	59	60
61	62	63	64	65	66	67	68	69	70
71	72	73	74	75	76	77	78	79	80
81	82	83	84	85	86	87	88	89	90
91	92	93	94	95	96	97	98	99	100

You will need a hundred square like this one.

Step 1. Cross off 1.

Step 2. Leave 2, but cross off all the other multiples of 2.

Step 3. Leave 3, but cross off all the other multiples of 3.

Step 4. 4 is already crossed off so go on to 5.
Leave 5 and cross off all the other multiples of 5.

Step 5. 6 is already crossed off so go on to 7.
Leave 7 and cross off all the other multiples of 7.

Step 6. The next number to leave will be 11.
Cross off the multiples of 11.

Step 7. Carry on this way until you have dealt with all the numbers.

Step 8. Check the list of numbers that are not crossed off.
They should be 2, 3, 5, 7, 11, 13, 17, 19, 23, 29, 31, 37, 41, 43, 47, 53, 59, 61, 67, 71, 73, 79, 83, 89 and 97.

These are called **prime numbers**.
A prime number has only two factors, 1 and the number itself.

A Prime Number Game.

This game is for any number of players.

You need one dice numbered 1 to 6 and two dice each numbered 4 to 9.

Roll the dice to decide the order in which you take turns.

The player with the highest total goes first.

Rules

A player rolls all three dice.

The player then multiplies the numbers on two of the dice, and adds **or** subtracts the number on the third dice.

If the player can make a prime number one point is scored.

The first player to score seven points is the winner.

Example:

Possible arrangements are:

$(7 \times 5) - 2 = 33$ As 33 is not a prime number there is no score.

$(7 \times 5) + 2 = 37$ 37 is a prime number so the player scores one point.

Some other possible ways of making a prime number with 7, 5 and 2 are:

$(5 \times 2) - 7 = 3$ $(5 \times 2) + 7 = 17$ $(7 \times 2) + 5 = 19$

Play the game several times.

Variation

Score one point for **every** prime number you can make with your three numbers, using the same rules as above.

How many lines? An investigation.

The object of this investigation is to try to find out how many lines are needed when each of a given number of points on a circle is joined to every other given point.

For example:

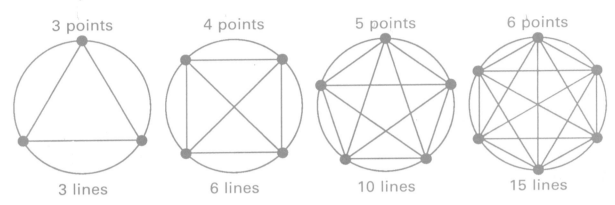

3 points	4 points	5 points	6 points
3 lines	6 lines	10 lines	15 lines

1   Draw a circle and mark any seven points on the circumference.
    Join each point to every other point, counting them as you do so.
    How many lines did you draw? (**Not** counting the circle!)

2   Repeat question 1 but with eight points instead of seven.

3   Counting so many lines can be boring so let's try to find an easier method.

    We will start with nine points.
    The first point must be joined to 8 others.
    The second point is already joined to the first one so must be joined to 7 others.
    The third point is already joined to the first and second points.
    It must be joined to 6 others

    Continuing like this we will find the total number of lines is:
    8 + 7 + 6 + 5 + 4 + 3 + 2 + 1 or 36.

    Use this method to check the answers in the examples at the top of the page and also your answers to questions 1 and 2.

4   If *n* is the number of points then the number of lines is $\frac{1}{2} \times n \times (n - 1)$.

    Check that this rule works for all the previous results.

5   Use the method in question 3 to find the number of lines if there are:

    (a)   12 points   (b)   15 points   (c)   20 points

Factors and common factors.

Since 4 × 3 = 12, 4 and 3 are
factors, or **divisors**, of 12.

$$\begin{array}{r} 4 \\ \times\ 3 \\ \hline 12 \end{array}$$

$$\begin{array}{r} 6 \\ \times\ 2 \\ \hline 12 \end{array}$$

$$\begin{array}{r} 12 \\ \times\ 1 \\ \hline 12 \end{array}$$

The factors of 12 are 1, 2, 3, 4, 6 and 12.

Is 10 a factor of 12?
Why or why not?

Factors of 18
1, 2, 3, 6, 9, 18

Factors of 24
1, 2, 3, 4, 6, 8, 12, 24

1, 2, 3 and 6 are factors of both 18 and 24.
They are called **common factors**, or **common divisors**, of 18 and 24.
6 is the highest number that will divide into 18 and 24 without leaving a
remainder. So the **highest common factor** of 18 and 24 is 6.

1   List all the factors.

 (a) 3   (b) 8   (c) 9   (d) 12   (e) 17   (f) 16

 (g) 19   (h) 21   (i) 20   (j) 22   (k) 23   (l) 25

 (m) 26   (n) 27   (o) 28   (p) 30   (q) 32   (r) 36

2   List all the common factors.

 (a) 8, 12   (b) 6, 8   (c) 7, 10   (d) 8, 24   (e) 15, 25

 (f) 10, 12   (g) 9, 18   (h) 9, 12   (i) 15, 18   (j) 10, 20

 (k) 16, 24   (l) 12, 16   (m) 15, 20   (n) 24, 36   (o) 16, 18

3   Give the highest common factor.

 (a) 9, 12   (b) 10, 35   (c) 8, 12   (d) 9, 24   (e) 14, 35

 (f) 18, 36   (g) 16, 20   (h) 16, 48   (i) 18, 45   (j) 18, 42

4   Copy this dot graph on to squared paper, then complete it for all the numbers up to 24.

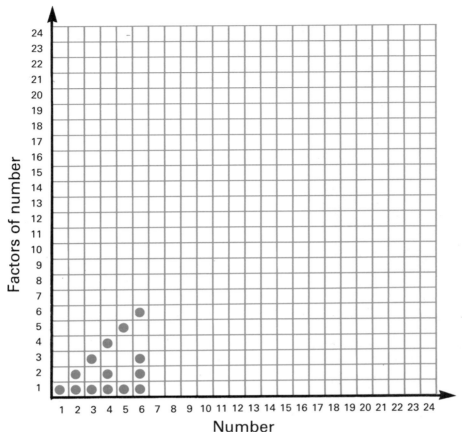

Number

Use your completed graph to answer the following questions.

5   How many factors does:
(a) 12 have?   (b) 18 have?

6   Which number has the most factors?

7   Which numbers have exactly 3 factors?

8   A prime number has exactly two factors. Which numbers on your graph are prime numbers?

9   (a) Use your graph to find numbers that are common factors of 12 and 18.
(b) What is the highest common factor of 12 and 18?

10   What else can you find out from your graph?

Multiplying larger numbers.

9364
9364
9364
9364
9364
9364
9364
9364

With a number of
5 digits or more we
use a gap to separate
the thousands from the
hundreds: 74 912.

Step 1. Multiply the units by 8.
Regroup 32 units as 3 tens
and 2 units.

```
  9364
×    8
     2
 3
```

Step 2. Multiply the tens by 8.
Add in the 3 tens from **Step 1**.
Regroup the 51 tens as
5 hundreds and 1 ten.

```
  9364
×    8
    12
 5 3
```

Step 3. Multiply the hundreds by 8.
Add in the 5 hundreds from
Step 2.
Regroup the 29 hundreds as
2 thousands and 9 hundreds.

```
  9364
×    8
   912
 2 5 3
```

Step 4. Multiply the thousands by 8.
Add in the 2 thousands from
Step 3.

```
  9364
×    8
 74912
 2 5 3
```

Other examples.

```
 37 824          53 296
×     6         ×     4
226 944         213 184
 44  12          1 1  3 2
```

Work these out.

1 (a)   3274   (b)   9106   (c)   3582   (d)   7136
       ×   5   ×   4   ×   6   ×   3

   (e)   52 816   (f)   39 428   (g)   74 385   (h)   60 342
       ×   4   ×   2   ×   3   ×   5

2 (a) **258 × 6**   (b) **423 × 9**   (c) **8 × 7421**
   (d) **3506 × 7**   (e) **5106 × 5**   (f) **4 × 39 174**

3 (a) How many pictures can you take
        with 6 rolls of this film?

   (b) What is the total price of 4 rolls of
        film?

4 (a) How much for
        7 of these cars?
   (b) How much for 5 of them?

5 A book has 12 685 words in it.
   How many words in: (a) 9 books?
                        (b) 6 books?

6 A house was built with 9876 bricks.
   How many bricks were needed to build:

   (a) 4 houses?
   (b) 8 houses?

7 A steel works agrees to provide a shipyard with 13 470 tonnes of steel
   a year. What is the number of tonnes provided in:
   (a) 2 years?   (b) 7 years?   (c) 9 years?

> Use your answer to question 8 (a) to write down
> the answers to questions (b) and (c).
> You do not need to multiply by 18 and 27 if
> you find the shortcut.

8 Multiply.

   (a)   12 345 679   (b)   12 345 679   (c)   12 345 679
       ×   9   ×   18   ×   27

Dividing into three and four-digit numbers

Let's revise division of a 3-digit number.

$3\overline{)442}$

Now use the same method for dividing a 4-digit number.

$5\overline{)3512}$

Step 1. Divide the hundreds.
Subtract.

$$
\begin{array}{r}
1 \\
3\overline{)442} \\
-300 \\
\hline
142
\end{array}
$$

Step 2. Divide the tens.
(14 tens ÷ 3)
Subtract.

$$
\begin{array}{r}
14 \\
3\overline{)442} \\
-300 \\
\hline
142 \\
-120 \\
\hline
22
\end{array}
$$

Step 3. Divide the units.
(22 units ÷ 3)
Subtract.

$$
\begin{array}{r}
147 \text{ R1} \\
3\overline{)442} \\
-300 \\
\hline
142 \\
-120 \\
\hline
22 \\
-21 \\
\hline
1
\end{array}
$$

Step 1. Divide the thousands.
There are not enough
thousands.

$5\overline{)3512}$

Step 2. Divide the hundreds.
(35 hundreds ÷ 5)
Subtract.

$$
\begin{array}{r}
7 \\
5\overline{)3512} \\
-3500 \\
\hline
12
\end{array}
$$

Step 3. Divide the tens.
There are not enough tens.

$$
\begin{array}{r}
70 \\
5\overline{)3512} \\
-3500 \\
\hline
12
\end{array}
$$

Step 4. Divide the units.
(12 units ÷ 5)
Subtract.

$$
\begin{array}{r}
702 \text{ R2} \\
5\overline{)3512} \\
-3500 \\
\hline
12 \\
-10 \\
\hline
2
\end{array}
$$

1 (a) $3\overline{)521}$ (b) $6\overline{)719}$ (c) $3\overline{)926}$ (d) $3\overline{)742}$ (e) $2\overline{)725}$

(f) $5\overline{)653}$ (g) $3\overline{)842}$ (h) $4\overline{)664}$ (i) $3\overline{)500}$ (j) $8\overline{)976}$

(k) $6\overline{)£8.34}$ (l) $6\overline{)£6.42}$ (m) $4\overline{)£8.32}$ (n) $8\overline{)£9.04}$ (o) $4\overline{)£8.28}$

(p) $4\overline{)1527}$ (q) $6\overline{)3215}$ (r) $8\overline{)4159}$ (s) $5\overline{)3293}$ (t) $8\overline{)7261}$

2 (a) $4526 \div 7$ (b) $3456 \div 9$ (c) $1394 \div 6$ (d) $2498 \div 9$ (e) $1645 \div 7$

(f) $4173 \div 5$ (g) $3818 \div 6$ (h) $3040 \div 4$ (i) $2815 \div 4$ (j) $2882 \div 4$

(k) $1675 \div 7$ (l) $3416 \div 2$ (m) $9314 \div 9$ (n) $5151 \div 6$ (o) $5436 \div 6$

It is easy to forget to write zeros in quotients.

No!

If you estimate first you may not make that mistake.
Here's a way to estimate a quotient.

Step 1. Find the first digit of the quotient.

$$\begin{array}{r} 9 \\ 3\overline{)2712} \end{array}$$

Step 2. Write zeros in *all* remaining places.

$$\begin{array}{r} 900 \\ 3\overline{)2712} \end{array} \leftarrow \text{estimate}$$

Step 3. Complete the division.

$$\begin{array}{r} 904 \\ 3\overline{)2712} \\ -2700 \\ \hline 12 \\ -12 \\ \hline 0 \end{array}$$

Step 4. Compare with the estimate. The answer is close to the estimate.

3 **Estimate. Then find each quotient and remainder.**

(a) $5\overline{)512}$ (b) $4\overline{)831}$ (c) $6\overline{)362}$ (d) $2\overline{)157}$ (e) $3\overline{)919}$

(f) $6\overline{)7153}$ (g) $2\overline{)9674}$ (h) $5\overline{)3517}$ (i) $8\overline{)2403}$ (j) $6\overline{)5418}$

Division puzzles.

You may use a calculator.

1   Using any three of the four digits (6, 7, 8 and 9) make a number that can be divided exactly by:

(a) **6**   (b) **2**   (c) **3**   (d) **4**

Your four answers must all be different.

For example: (9 × 8) − 6 = 72 − 6 = 66.
66 is divisible by 6. This could be an answer to (a).
(It could also be an answer to (b) or (c)! But don't forget, you can't use the same answer more than once.)

2   (a)   Can you make a number, using any three of the same four digits (6, 7, 8 and 9) that is divisible by 2, 3, 4 **and** 6?

(b)   Find any other solutions there are to (a).

3   Can you make a number that is divisible by 7:

(a)   using three of the same four digits?

(b)   using all four digits?

4   Some arrangements of any three of the digits result in numbers that are divisible by 3. There are twenty-four possible 3-digit numbers, using 9, 6, 8, and 7. List them and check which ones can be divided exactly by 3.

5   'Any number is divisible by 3 if the sum of its digits is divisible by 3.'

Use your calculator to check this statement for some numbers with:

(a) **4 digits**   (b) **5 digits**   (c) **6 digits**

Ask your teacher for a day off school if you find a whole number that breaks this rule!

Dividing by a two-digit number.

We divide by a two-digit number the same
way that we divide by a one-digit number.
Here are the multiplication facts for 24.
Use them to do a division problem.

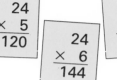

$$\begin{array}{r} 24 \\ \times\ 0 \\ \hline 0 \end{array} \quad \begin{array}{r} 24 \\ \times\ 1 \\ \hline 24 \end{array} \quad \begin{array}{r} 24 \\ \times\ 2 \\ \hline 48 \end{array} \quad \begin{array}{r} 24 \\ \times\ 3 \\ \hline 72 \end{array}$$

Example $24\overline{)786}$

$$\begin{array}{r} 24 \\ \times\ 4 \\ \hline 96 \end{array} \quad \begin{array}{r} 24 \\ \times\ 5 \\ \hline 120 \end{array} \quad \begin{array}{r} 24 \\ \times\ 6 \\ \hline 144 \end{array} \quad \begin{array}{r} 24 \\ \times\ 7 \\ \hline 168 \end{array} \quad \begin{array}{r} 24 \\ \times\ 8 \\ \hline 192 \end{array} \quad \begin{array}{r} 24 \\ \times\ 9 \\ \hline 216 \end{array}$$

Discuss each step with a friend.

Step 1.   Not enough hundreds. (Only 7.)

$24\overline{)786}$

Step 2.   Think of 7 hundreds and 8 tens as 78 tens.
Divide. (78 ÷ 24 = 3)
Subtract 3 lots of 24. (3 × 24 = 72)

$$\begin{array}{r} 3 \\ 24\overline{)786} \\ -\ 720 \\ \hline 6 \end{array}$$ Remember: these are 72 tens.
tens left over

$$\begin{array}{r} 24 \\ \times\ 3 \\ \hline 72 \end{array}$$

Step 3.   Add the units to the left-over tens.

$$\begin{array}{r} 3 \\ 24\overline{)786} \\ -\ 720 \\ \hline 66 \end{array}$$

Step 4.   Think of the 6 tens and 6 units as 66 units.
Divide. (66 ÷ 24 = 2)
Subtract 2 lots of 24. (2 × 24 = 48)

$$\begin{array}{r} 32 \\ 24\overline{)786} \\ -\ 720 \\ \hline 66 \\ -\ 48 \\ \hline 18 \end{array}$$

$$\begin{array}{r} 24 \\ \times\ 2 \\ \hline 48 \end{array}$$

Step 5.   Put the remaining units with the answer.

$$\begin{array}{r} 32\ \text{R}18 \\ 24\overline{)786} \\ -\ 720 \\ \hline 66 \\ -\ 48 \\ \hline 18 \end{array}$$

Use the given multiplication facts to help you with the divisions.

1

| 27 × 0 = 0 | 27 × 1 = 27 | 27 × 2 = 54 | 27 × 3 = 81 | 27 × 4 = 108 | 27 × 5 = 135 | 27 × 6 = 162 | 27 × 7 = 189 | 27 × 8 = 216 | 27 × 9 = 243 |

(a) 27)864 (b) 27)962 (c) 27)298 (d) 27)513 (e) 27)729

(f) 27)803 (g) 27)958 (h) 27)742 (i) 27)690 (j) 27)899

2

| 19 × 0 = 0 | 19 × 1 = 19 | 19 × 2 = 38 | 19 × 3 = 57 | 19 × 4 = 76 | 19 × 5 = 95 | 19 × 6 = 114 | 19 × 7 = 133 | 19 × 8 = 152 | 19 × 9 = 171 |

(a) 19)258 (b) 19)374 (c) 19)526 (d) 19)675 (e) 19)400

(f) 19)783 (g) 19)877 (h) 19)370 (i) 19)964 (j) 19)587

To estimate the quotient, find the greatest multiple of 57 that is less than (or equal to) 315.

```
    5
57)315
```

| 57 × 0 = 0 | 57 × 1 = 57 | 57 × 2 = 114 | 57 × 3 = 171 | 57 × 4 = 228 |
| 57 × 5 = 285 | 57 × 6 = 342 | 57 × 7 = 399 | 57 × 8 = 456 | 57 × 9 = 513 |

3 Estimate each quotient. Then divide.

(a) 57)367   (b) 57)107   (c) 57)167

(d) 57)395   (e) 57)841   (f) 57)564

(g) 57)631   (h) 57)459   (i) 57)483

More about dividing by a two-digit number.

In the questions on page 86 you were given all the multiplication facts. Here you will have to work out your own multiplication facts as you divide. The examples show how to use rounding to decide which multiplication facts are needed.

Example 1   32)870

Step 1. Round the divisor to the nearest 10. Think about dividing by 30.

30
32)870

Step 2. Think about the multiplication facts for 30. Divide 30 into the 87 tens.

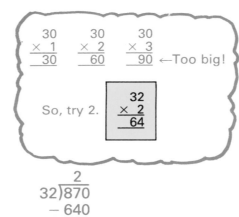

30	30	30
× 1	× 2	× 3
30	60	90 ←Too big!

So, try 2.

```
 32
×  2
 64
```

Step 3. Think about the multiplication facts for 30. Divide 30 into 230.

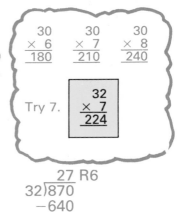

30	30	30
× 6	× 7	× 8
180	210	240

Try 7.

```
 32
×  7
224
```

```
        2
  32)870
   −640
    230
```

```
       27 R6
  32)870
   −640
    230
   −224
      6
```

Example 2.   36)754

Step 1.

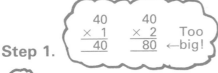

40	40	
× 1	× 2	Too
40	80	←big!

40

```
      ①
  36)754
   −360
    394
```

Since 39 is more than 36 we need to use

```
 36
×  2
 72
```

Step 2.

```
        2
  36)754
   −720
     34
```

Step 3.

```
       20 R34
  36)754
   −720
     34
```

1 To what number would you round the divisor? You don't need to do the divisions!

(a) 23)783   (b) 49)956   (c) 71)803   (d) 36)916   (e) 54)642

2 Divide.

(a) 18)927   (b) 40)900   (c) 61)765   (d) 16)699   (e) 34)742

(f) 33)683   (g) 23)374   (h) 43)894   (i) 47)963   (j) 42)826

3

(a) How many rolls of film would you have to buy to take 110 pictures?
(b) What would be the total price?

4

(a) How many boxes of screws would you have to buy to get 600 screws?
(b) What would be the total price?

5

A business woman has 724 letters to post.
(a) How many packets of envelopes does she need?
(b) What will be the total price?

6

There are 21 children at a party. Each child is to have 10 chocolates.
(a) How many chocolates are needed?
(b) How many boxes of chocolates are needed?
(c) What will be the total price?

The four operations with brackets (3).

Remember to complete the calculations in the brackets first.

$(3897 - 3193) \div 64 = 11$

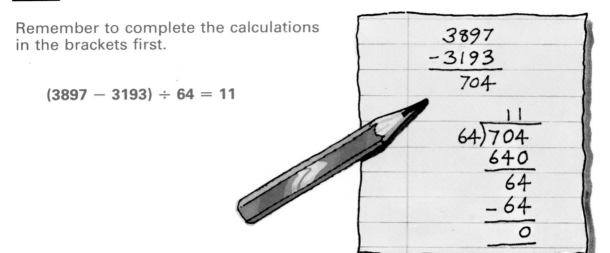

1   **Work these out.**

(a) $(258 + 367) - 367 = $ __

(b) $(582 + 453) - 453 = $ __

(c) $(942 + 365) + 218 = $ __

(d) $942 + (365 + 218) = $ __

(e) $(782 - 256) - 142 = $ __

(f) $782 - (256 - 142) = $ __

(g) $(512 \div 16) \div 4 = $ __

(h) $512 \div (16 \div 4) = $ __

(i) $(56 \times 25) \div 5 = $ __

(j) $(4 \times 39) \div 39 = $ __

(k) $(444 \div 74) + 125 = $ __

(l) $238 \times (252 \div 28) = $ __

(m) $(1024 - 512) \div 32 = $ __

(n) $1024 - (512 \div 32) = $ __

(o) $(238 \times 5) + 17 = $ __

(p) $238 \times (5 + 17) = $ __

2

NEWCASTLE

438 km

316 km

OXFORD

PLYMOUTH

If you average 58 kilometres per hour, how long will it take you to drive from Newcastle to Plymouth?

3   An apple grower ordered 960 trees. If 42 trees are planted in each row, how many rows can be planted?
How many trees will be left over?

4   A farmer wants to build a fence that is 912 metres long. If the posts are 3 metres apart, how many will be needed?
(*Careful!* The answer is not 304.)

Tessellations.

You need some squared paper.

1

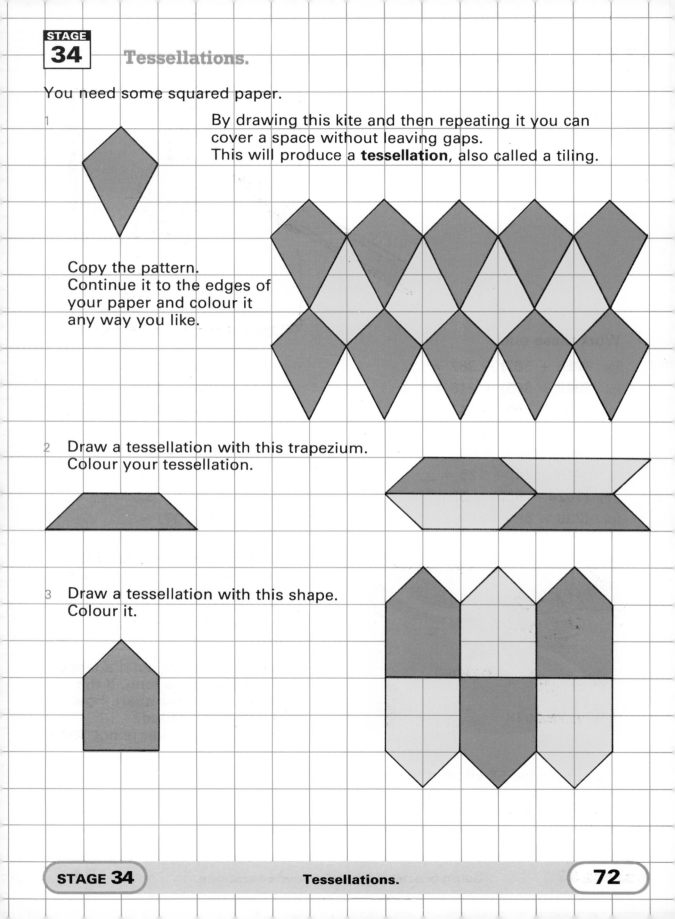

By drawing this kite and then repeating it you can cover a space without leaving gaps.
This will produce a **tessellation**, also called a tiling.

Copy the pattern.
Continue it to the edges of your paper and colour it any way you like.

2 Draw a tessellation with this trapezium.
Colour your tessellation.

3 Draw a tessellation with this shape.
Colour it.

You need some squared paper for these tessellations.
You can draw many different tessellations using shapes
made by joining squares.

Continue the tessellations shown and colour them in your own way.
Colour any shapes that touch with different colours.

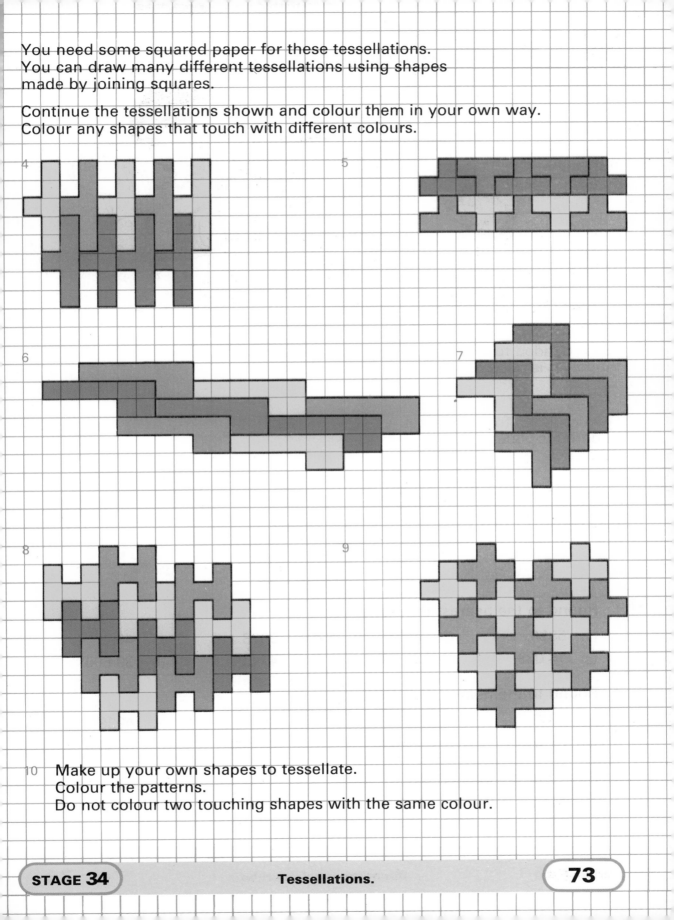

4

5

6

7

8

9

10   Make up your own shapes to tessellate.
      Colour the patterns.
      Do not colour two touching shapes with the same colour.

Rounding whole numbers.

Sometimes approximate numbers are used. The exact price of the car is not £6000, but £5835. The exact price was **rounded to the nearest thousand**.

5835 rounded to the nearest thousand is 6000.

5835 rounded to the nearest hundred is 5800.

When the number is halfway between, round up.

5835 rounded to the nearest ten is 5840.

1   **Round to the nearest thousand.**

(a)	**5826**	(b)	**6374**	(c)	**9028**	(d)	**4691**
(e)	**14 039**	(f)	**28 243**	(g)	**47 500**	(h)	**39 800**

2   **Round to the nearest hundred.**

(a)	**7346**	(b)	**9214**	(c)	**3560**	(d)	**4938**
(e)	**29 643**	(f)	**75 385**	(g)	**29 580**	(h)	**86 950**

3   **Round to the nearest ten.**

(a)	**4794**	(b)	**3333**	(c)	**9308**	(d)	**4567**
(e)	**37**	(f)	**724**	(g)	**10 899**	(h)	**11 111**

Here is a method for rounding.

Step 1. Find the place to which you are rounding.

Step 2. Look at the next digit to the right.

Step 3. If that digit is 5 or greater, round up. If that digit is less than 5, round down.

Round to the nearest thousand.

578 341
  ↑

578 341
  ↑ ↓

578 341
  ↑ ↓

3 is less than 5.
Round down: 578 000.

4 Round:

(a) 35 928 to the nearest ten.

(b) 26 753 to the nearest thousand.

(c) 84 219 to the nearest hundred.

(d) 59 037 to the nearest thousand.

(e) 482 961 to the nearest hundred.

(f) 357 281 to the nearest ten.

(g) 426 350 to the nearest hundred.

(h) 291 784 to the nearest thousand.

5 Pretend you are a newspaper reporter. Write a headline for each fact, rounding the numbers.

(a) The city council had a budget of £598 382.

(b) Concorde reached 2198 km/h during a recent flight.

(c) Last night 42 056 people went to Wembley Stadium to see a pop concert.

6 Sherlock Holmes is trying to guess which Digits are missing from the number. Study the clues and find the number.
Clue 1: if you round to the nearest thousand you get 70 000.
Clue 2: the number of tens is one more than the number of units.
The number is the greatest possible to satisfy both clue 1 and clue 2.

7 Set problems like question 6 for your friends to solve.

Metric and imperial units.

Here is some useful information.

≈ means 'is approximately equal to'.

1 inch (in) ≈ 25.4 mm = 2.54 cm
1 foot (ft) ≈ 0.3 m
1 yard (yd) ≈ 0.91 m   1 m ≈ 1.09 yd
1 mile ≈ 1.61 km   1 km ≈ 0.62 miles

1 pint (pt) ≈ 0.57 litres   1 litre ≈ 1.76 pt

1 pound (lb) ≈ 0.45 kg   1 kg ≈ 2.2 lb

To change inches to centimetres
I multiply by 2.54

To change centimetres to inches
I divide by 2.54

1   State which of the two units is the greater.

   (a)   inch or centimetre   (b)   yard or metre   (c)   mile or kilometre

   (d)   foot or metre   (e)   pint or litre   (f)   pound or kilogram

2   Use your calculator and the relationships given at the top of the page to
     find these approximations. Give your answers correct to one decimal place.

   (a)   17 in ≈ __ cm   (b)   16 yd ≈ __ m   (c)   23 ft ≈ __ m

   (d)   18 cm ≈ __ in   (e)   4 miles ≈ __ km   (f)   6 km ≈ __ miles

   (g)   56 m ≈ __ yd   (h)   12 litres ≈ __ pt   (i)   29 lb ≈ __ kg

3   Work with some friends to write a report on how time could be metricated.
     Start with a year of 10 months. A month may be any length you wish. List
     the main problems in metricating time.

1   Carol wants to dance with a boy of average weight. Which of these should she choose?

Toby, who weighs 58 kg
Imran, who weighs 29 000 g
Charlie, who weighs 100 kg

2   Gary is 5 feet 10 inches tall. He would like to dance with a tall girl, but one who is shorter than he is. Which of these could he choose?

Nia, height 152 cm
Lucy, height 174 cm
Linda, height 180 cm

3   Gary is going to buy a box of chocolates for his girlfriend's birthday present. He cannot afford to spend more than £6. Which box should he choose?

4   Carol has quite a slim waist. She says she will next dance with the boy who gives the best approximate measurement of it. Who will she dance with?

Winston says 25 cm
Graham says 80 cm
Momodu says 50 cm

1 stone (st) = 14 pounds (lb)

5   Last year Carol weighed 6 stone 12 pounds. Her weight has increased by 11 pounds. How much does she weigh now?

6   Gary used to weigh 10 stones exactly. During his training for the Great North Run, he lost 2 kilograms in weight.
    (a)   What was his weight loss in pounds? (1 kg ≈ 2.2 lb)
    (b)   What was his weight at the start of the Great North Run?

7   Copy and complete the following sentences, naming something that is approximately the given measurement. The first one is done as an example.
    (a)   A farmyard animal with a height of about 50 cm is a *chicken*. (Other possible answers are duck, small dog, etc.)
    (b)   A girl with a weight of 50 kg might be about __ years old.
    (c)   You could run 50 yards in about __ seconds.
    (d)   If 50 lb of meat was used for school dinners it would be enough for about __ pupils.
    (e)   To cycle 50 kilometres would take about __ hours.

Congruent shapes.

These girls are identical twins. The picture of one would fit exactly on the other.

These three cards could be stacked so that each card fits exactly on the other two.

Shapes that exactly fit one another are called **congruent shapes**.

Tracings of congruent shapes will exactly go over one another.

1   **Name any pairs of shapes that are congruent.**

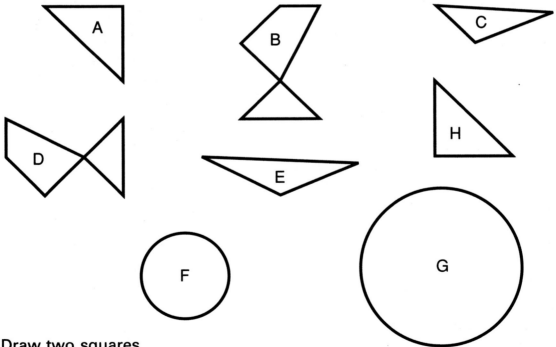

2   **Draw two squares**

   (a)   **that are congruent**   (b)   **that are not congruent.**

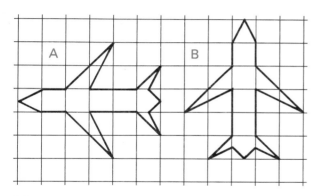

A and B are exactly the
same size and shape.
They are congruent.
The tracing of one will
exactly fit the other.

Match the congruent shapes. Each number can be matched to a letter.

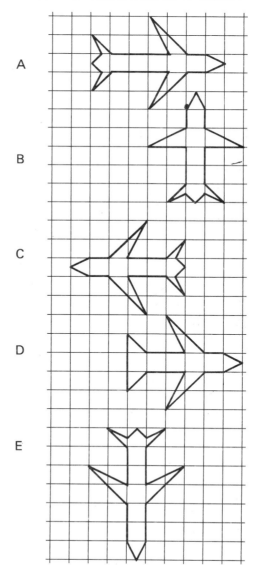

1

2

3

4

5

A

B

C

D

E

6 Jessica has three rubber stamps.
   She used them to make the
   red shapes shown below.
   Could the blue shapes have been
   made with the same stamps?
   Answer "Yes" or "No".
   (*Hint:* make tracings
   to help you.)

(a)

(b)

(c)

(d)

(e)

(f)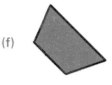

(g)

(h)

(i)

(j)

Triangles.

Drawing triangles.

Here is how to draw a triangle with sides of 8 cm, 6 cm and 4 cm.

Step 1. Draw a line and mark two points on it (A and B) 8 cm apart.

Step 2. Set your compasses to a radius of 6 cm. With centre A, make an arc with radius 6 cm.

Step 3. Set your compasses to a radius of 4 cm. With centre B, make an arc to cross the other arc (at C).

Step 4. Join A and B to C. Triangle ABC has the required measurements.

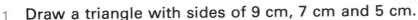

1 Draw a triangle with sides of 9 cm, 7 cm and 5 cm.

2 Draw a triangle ABC with these sides:
AB = 10 cm; BC = 8.5 cm; CA = 6 cm.
Measure angles A, B and C.

3 Draw a triangle CDE with these sides:
CD = 11 cm; DE = 7.8 cm; EC = 8.1 cm.
Measure angles C, D and E.

4 Draw an isosceles triangle with the base 7 cm and the two equal sides 6.6 cm.
Measure the three angles.

5 Find a friend who has also drawn these triangles.
Each of you trace your own triangles.

Exchange your tracings. Check that your friend's tracings fit over your triangles.
You may need to turn over the tracing paper.

Congruent triangles.

These two triangles are congruent. The parts that fit each other are called **corresponding parts**.
The tracing of the triangle ABC can be fitted exactly to the triangle MNO.

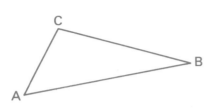
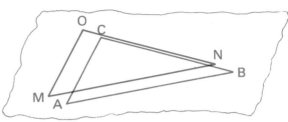

We can list the corresponding parts of the above triangles like this:

Corresponding sides
AB = MN
BC = NO
CA = OM

Corresponding angles
∠ A = ∠ M
∠ B = ∠ N
∠ C = ∠ O

Corresponding parts are equal to each other.

Find a way to fit one congruent triangle to the other.
You should use tracing paper and you may need to turn your tracings over to make them fit.
Then list the corresponding parts.

1
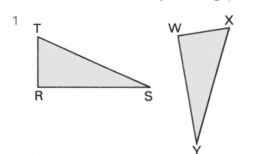

2
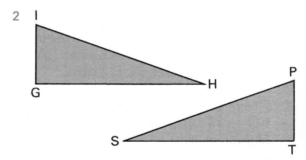

3
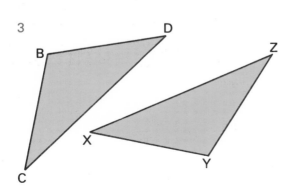

4
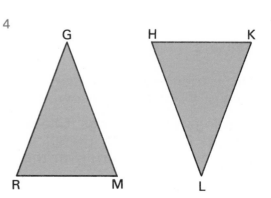

5 There are two congruent triangles
in this shape. Find them and list
the corresponding parts.

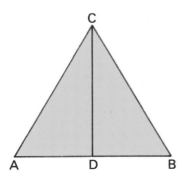

6 Here is a triangle with angles of
50°, 60° and 70°. Draw a triangle
that has the same size angles but
is not congruent to this one.

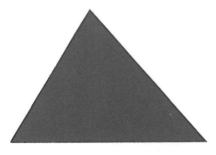

7 Here is a triangle with sides of
5 cm, 6 cm and 8 cm. Can you
draw a triangle that has sides the
same length but is not congruent
to this one?

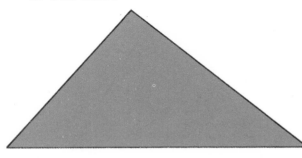

8 Draw two triangles that are *not* congruent, but both with a right angle and
with one side of 6 cm and one side of 8 cm.

Three kinds of triangle

A triangle with all three sides equal is called an **equilateral triangle**.

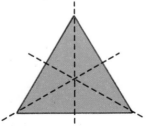

The three angles are equal.
It has three lines of symmetry.

A triangle with two sides equal is called an **isosceles triangle**.

Two angles are equal.
It has one line of symmetry.

A triangle with no sides equal is called a **scalene triangle**.

No angles are equal.
It has no lines of symmetry.

1   The dashed line is a line of symmetry.

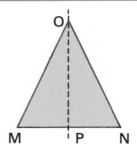

(a)   Which triangle is congruent to triangle OPM?

(b)   Which line corresponds to OM?

(c)   Which angle is equal to ∠M?

2   Trace this equilateral triangle and its three lines of symmetry.

(a)   Fold your triangle so that AB fits on AC.
This will show AB = AC.

(b)   Open out your triangle.
Fold it to show AB = BC.

(c)   How do you know that AC = BC?
(You *don't* need to fold the triangle this time.)

3   Name five different triangles that are congruent to triangle CPA.

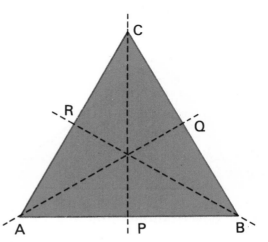

A pie chart.

The pie chart shows the results of a school survey.
For example, it shows that football and cricket were the favourite sports.
Each of these was chosen by $\frac{1}{4}$ of the pupils.

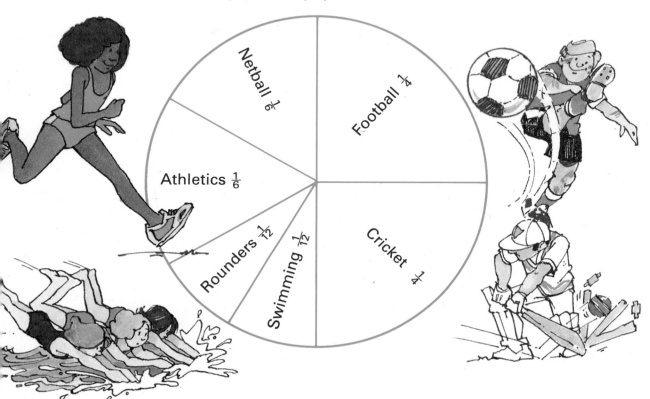

Netball $\frac{1}{6}$

Football $\frac{1}{4}$

Athletics $\frac{1}{6}$

Rounders $\frac{1}{12}$

Swimming $\frac{1}{12}$

Cricket $\frac{1}{4}$

1   There were 624 pupils in the school. Only 208 were in the survey. How many were not in the survey?

2   What fraction of the pupils were surveyed? Give your answer in the simplest form.
(Remember question 1.)

3   Thirteen pupils conducted the survey of the 208 pupils. What was the average number of pupils questioned by each?

4   During the lunch hour, the 13 pupils each questioned 9 other pupils. How many pupils were questioned during the lunch hour?

5   Did more pupils choose football or swimming?

6   What fraction of the pupils did not choose football?

7   Find the total fraction of pupils who chose athletics and swimming.

8   Find the total fraction of pupils who chose a sport other than netball or football.

Pie charts.

There are 360° in a full turn through a circle.
If the circle is used to represent 24 hours,
then 1 hour is represented by 15° because

$$360° \div 24 = 15°$$

Each of the 24 angles at the centre
of the circle is 15°.

> The shaded part is called a **sector**.

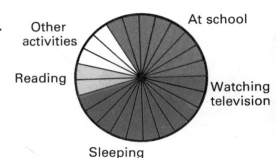

1   **Copy and complete:**

Number of hours	1	2	3	4	5	6	7	8	9	10	11	12
Number of degrees	15											

Number of hours	13	14	15	16	17	18	19	20	21	22	23	24
Number of degrees												

2   The pie chart shows how Sue spent a day.
How long did she spend:
(a) watching television?
(b) sleeping?
(c) at school?
(d) reading?
(e) doing other activities?

Other activities
At school
Reading
Watching television
Sleeping

3   There are 180 pupils at a school.
(a) How many degrees are there in the
angle that represents 1 pupil?
(b) The pie chart shows how they
travel to school.
Measure the angles, then
copy and complete the table.

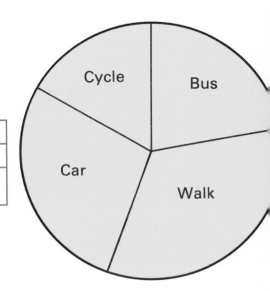

Cycle
Bus
Car
Walk

	Car	Bus	Walk	Cycle
Angle				
Number of children				

4   Decide how you spend a day.
Draw a pie chart to represent it.

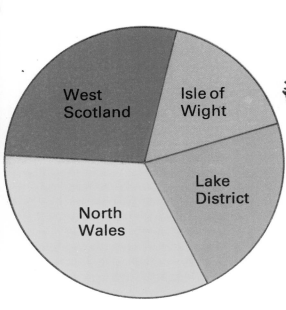

90 children were going on a school camping holiday. They were asked where they would most like to go. The pie chart shows the children's choices.

Each pupil's choice is represented by $\frac{360°}{90}$ or 4°.

5 Measure each of the four angles at the centre of the circle.
Copy and complete this table.

	Isle of Wight	Lake District	North Wales	West Scotland
Angle				
Number of children				

6 How many children would be represented by:

(a) 20°?   (b) 48°?   (c) 92°?   (d) 116°?   (e) 140°?

7 How many degrees would represent these numbers of children:

(a) 13?   (b) 33?   (c) 42?   (d) 57?   (e) 69?

8 (a) If there had been 80 children instead of 90, how many degrees would represent each child?

(b) Copy and complete this table to show the number of degrees that represent each child.

Number of children	40	60	72	100	144	150
Angle for each child						

Revision of percentage.

18% means 18 out of 100.

As a fraction 18% = $\frac{18}{100}$

In its lowest terms this is $\frac{9}{50}$

So 18% = $\frac{9}{50}$

By making the denominator of
a fraction into 100 we can change
the fraction into a percentage.

$\frac{7}{25} = \frac{7 \times 4}{25 \times 4} = \frac{28}{100} = 28\%$

18% is shaded.

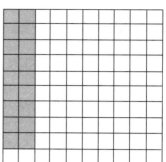

15% of £8 = £$\frac{15 \times 8}{100}$ = £$\frac{120}{100}$ = £1.20

The amount paid is £8 – £1.20 = £6.80

1 Write these percentages as fractions in their lowest terms:

   (a) 20%   (b) 50%   (c) 80%   (d) 91%   (e) 76%

2 Write these fractions as percentages:

   (a) $\frac{4}{25}$ (b) $\frac{19}{50}$ (c) $\frac{7}{10}$ (d) $\frac{4}{5}$ (e) $\frac{11}{20}$ (f) $\frac{3}{4}$

3 Calculate these amounts:

   (a) 10% of £25   (b) 5% of £80   (c) 30% of £20

   (d) 20% of £13   (e) 9% of £34   (f) 17% of £12

4

Calculate (i) the discount and (ii) the
amount paid for these items:

   (a) a dress costing £35

   (b) a pair of shoes costing £32

   (c) a blouse costing £26

Percentage with pie charts.

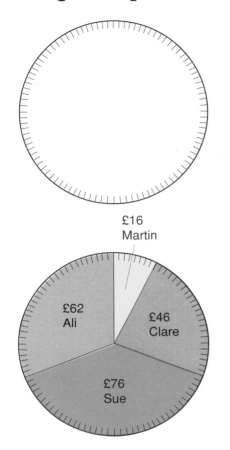

This circle has been divided into 100 equal parts, called sectors.
Each sector is 1% of the circle.

This pie chart shows how much money was collected by each person on a sponsored walk.
Altogether they collected £200
1% of £200 = £2
£16 is 8% of £200 and therefore is represented by 8 sectors.

1 In the pie chart above calculate the number of sectors that represent

(a) £46　(b) £76　(c) £62

2

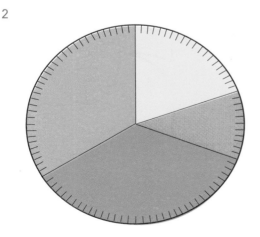

400 people were asked to state which colour they liked best out of red, blue, yellow and green.
20% chose yellow
35% chose red
34% chose blue.

(a) What percentage chose green?

(b) How many chose (i) yellow
(ii) red　(iii) blue　(iv) green?

Multiplying by 10 and 100.

Reminder

Here are the rules you learnt for multiplying by 10.

When you multiply by 10 write zero in the units place of the answer and then:
The units digit becomes the tens digit in the answer.
The tens digit becomes the hundreds digit in the answer.
The hundreds digit becomes the thousands digit in the answer.
The thousands digit becomes the ten thousands digit in the answer.

When multiplying by 10 we say that each digit is **promoted** (or moved) one place to the left.

$100 = 10 \times 10$

Multiplying by 100 is the same as multiplying by 10 and then multiplying by 10 again. Hence:

When you multiply by 100 write zero in the units and tens places of the answer and then:
The units digit becomes the hundreds digit in the answer.
The tens digit becomes the thousands digit in the answer.
The hundreds digit becomes the ten thousands digit in the answer.
The thousands digit becomes the hundred thousands digit in the answer.

When multiplying by 100 we say that each digit is **promoted** (or moved) two places to the left.

1 (a) $\begin{array}{r} 67 \\ \times\ 10 \\ \hline \end{array}$ (b) $\begin{array}{r} 41 \\ \times\ 10 \\ \hline \end{array}$ (c) $\begin{array}{r} 132 \\ \times\ 10 \\ \hline \end{array}$ (d) $\begin{array}{r} 2163 \\ \times\ 10 \\ \hline \end{array}$ (e) $\begin{array}{r} 3840 \\ \times\ 10 \\ \hline \end{array}$

2 (a) $\begin{array}{r} 52 \\ \times\ 100 \\ \hline \end{array}$ (b) $\begin{array}{r} 33 \\ \times\ 100 \\ \hline \end{array}$ (c) $\begin{array}{r} 105 \\ \times\ 100 \\ \hline \end{array}$ (d) $\begin{array}{r} 467 \\ \times\ 100 \\ \hline \end{array}$ (e) $\begin{array}{r} 1703 \\ \times\ 100 \\ \hline \end{array}$

Using inverses to divide by 10 and 100.

Division and multiplication are **inverse operations**.
Since 132 × 10 = 1320, it follows that 1320 ÷ 10 = 132

What number should we multiply by 10 to get 640?

? × 10 = 640
The answers is 64, so 640 ÷ 10 = 64.

In the same way we can divide by 100.
78 × 100 = 7800, so 7800 ÷ 100 = 78.
? × 100 = 7800.
The answer is 78, so 7800 ÷ 100 = 78.

Divide these by 10:

1 (a) **410**   (b) **780**   (c) **60**   (d) **1970**   (e) **3600**

Divide these by 100:

2 (a) **500**   (b) **6000**   (c) **4300**   (d) **91 600**   (e) **77 000**

3 Use a calculator to divide (i) by 10 and (ii) by 100.

   (a) **12 000**   (b) **34 600**   (c) **79 100**   (d) **284 000**

4 Look at your answers to questions 1, 2 and 3.
   Then copy and complete the following statements.

   A When you divide by 10 each digit moves one place to the ....

   B When you divide by 100 each digit moves .... places to ....

5 Find 1% of:

   (a) £200   (b) £4100   (c) 5800 m   (d) 94 000 kg

6 Use your results from question 5 to find:

   (a) 2% and   (b) 5% of the amounts given in that question.

Multiplying by 1000.

$1000 = 10 \times 10 \times 10 = 100 \times 10 = 10 \times 100.$

To multiply by 1000 you can:
    (a) multiply by 10, then by 10 again, then by 10 again
or (b) multiply by 100 and then by 10
or (c) multiply by 10 and then by 100.

Example
Multiply 78 by 1000.

(a) $78 \times 10 = 780$ $780 \times 10 = 7800$ $7800 \times 10 = 78\,000$

(b) $78 \times 100 = 7800$ $7800 \times 10 = 78\,000$

(c) $78 \times 10 = 780$ $780 \times 100 = 78\,000$

1   Use each of the three methods above to multiply:

   (a) **41 by 1000**   (b) **346 by 1000.**

2   Use any one of the three methods to multiply these numbers by 1000:

   (a) **9**   (b) **23**   (c) **138**   (d) **204**   (e) **100.**

3   Check that the following rule applies to all your answers to questions 1 and 2.
   When you multiply by 1000, write 0s in the units, tens and hundreds position and then
      the units digit becomes the thousands digit
      the tens digit becomes the ten thousands digit
      the hundreds digit becomes the hundred thousands digit

4   (a) **92 × 1000**   (b) **30 × 1000**   (c) **410 × 1000**

5    There are approximately 1000 seeds in every packet. How many seeds would there be in

   (a) **24 packets?**   (b) **107 packets?**   (c) **600 packets?**

Dividing by 1000.

Since 1000 = 10 × 10 × 10 = 100 × 10 = 10 × 100, we can divide by 1000 in these three ways:

   (a)   divide by 10, then by 10 again, then by 10 again

or (b)   divide by 100 and then by 10

or (c)   divide by 10 and then by 100.

Another method is to use the fact that multiplication and division are inverse operations.

? × 1000 = 79 000
The answer is 79, so 79 000 ÷ 1000 = 79

Which number should we multiply 1000 by to get 79 000?

1   Divide these by 1000:

   (a)   **7000**   (b) **10 000**   (c) **28 000**   (d) **163 000**

2   Use a calculator to divide these by 1000:

   (a)   **9000**   (b) **30 000**   (c) **101 000**   (d) **940 000**

3   Look at your answers to questions 1 and 2.
    Then copy and complete the following statements.

    A When you divide by 1000, each digit moves .... places to the ....

    B When you multiply by 1000 each digit moves .... places to the ....

4

1000 PINS

How many packets of pins if there are:

(a) **37 000 pins?**   (b) **214 000 pins?**
(c) **980 000 pins?**

Shortcuts for multiplication.

Tessa and Colin have thought of some shortcuts for multiplication.

Here's how I multiply by 5.

$5 = \frac{10}{2}$

Multiply by 10, then divide by 2.

Examples:

$$784 \times 5 = \frac{784 \times 10}{2}$$
$$= \frac{7840}{2}$$
$$= 3920$$

Here's how I multiply by 25.

$25 = \frac{100}{4}$

Multiply by 100, then divide by 4.

$$652 \times 25 = \frac{652 \times 100}{4}$$
$$= \frac{65\,200}{4}$$
$$= 16\,300$$

Here's how I multiply by 125.

$125 = \frac{1000}{8}$

Multiply by 1000, then divide by 8.

$$368 \times 125 = \frac{368 \times 1000}{8}$$
$$= \frac{368\,000}{8}$$
$$= 46\,000$$

Try Tessa's and Colin's methods to do these multiplications.
You will be able to do many of them in your head.

1 (a) 286×5 (b) 694×5 (c) 832×5 (d) 963×5

2 (a) 64×25 (b) 124×25 (c) 216×25 (d) 312×25

3 (a) 136×125 (b) 272×125 (c) 496×125 (d) 608×125

4 Try multiplying other numbers by 5, 25 and 125.
   You may find it easier in some cases to divide before multiplying.
   Do either first.

5 Try to invent some shortcuts of your own for division.